LANGUAGE
and
Woman's Place

*the text of this book is printed
on 100% recycled paper*

LANGUAGE
and
Woman's Place

ROBIN LAKOFF

HARPER COLOPHON BOOKS
Harper & Row, Publishers
New York, Evanston, San Francisco, London

Grateful acknowledgment is hereby made to Cambridge University Press for permission to reprint "Language and Woman's Place" by Robin Lakoff from *Language and Society*.

First HARPER COLOPHON edition published 1975.

LIBRARY OF CONGRESS CATALOG CARD NUMBER: 74–27493

STANDARD BOOK NUMBER: 06–090389–9

Designed by Eve Callahan

75 76 77 78 10 9 8 7 6 5 4 3 2 1

FOR ANDY

whose generation will, I hope, have transcended these issues
by the time it can read this book.

Contents

Preface

One can look at woman's position in our society from any number of points of view and gain enlightenment from each. In this book I have tried to see what we can learn about the way women view themselves and everyone's assumptions about the nature and role of women from the use of language in our culture, that is to say, the language used by and about women. While my reasons for taking this particular tack are based on my training in linguistics, I feel that such study is quite justifiable in its own terms. Language is more amenable to precise reproduction on paper and unambiguous analysis than are other forms of human behavior; if we tell someone he has done something sexist, we often don't know how to describe exactly what he's done so that we can argue meaningfully about the truth of that assertion: the evidence vanishes before it can be studied. But if we say to someone, "You said . . . , which is insulting to women," provided he agrees that he has made the statement, it is available and open to close analysis. Often, as psychoanalysis has shown in such detail, we say things without knowing their significance, but the fact that we have said them shows that there is more going on in our minds than we consciously take credit for. By looking at the way we customarily talk if we are women, or talk about women whoever we are, we can gain insight into the way we feel—about ourselves, about women— through close analysis of what we say and how we say it until in the end we can ask and perhaps even answer the question: *Why* did I say it? It is my hope, then, to look at some of these linguistic issues and see what they tell us.

The ideas that are discussed in the book are the result of many hours of mind-stretching and insightful discussion and argument with many people, mention of whose names here is scarcely a just reward for what each has contributed to my thinking. First of all, in both time and importance, George Lakoff has been my teacher, adviser, and friend, linguistically and otherwise, for many years; most of what I know about language can be traced to him. I have also learned by having to argue him out of male-chauvinist ways and assumptions many times over the years; probably I would never have started thinking about the questions posed here had he not forced me to defend myself in arguments about linguistic sexism.

Many of my colleagues and friends have also been helpful; let me single out a few for mention, though many others have been helpful as well, Charlotte Baker, Wallace Chafe, Herb and Eve Clark, Louise Cherry, Alan Dershowitz, Richard Diebold, James Fox, David Green, Georgia Green, John and Jenny Gumperz, Dell Hymes, Mary Ritchie Key, John and Sally Lawler, Susan Matisoff, James D. McCawley, Michelle Rosaldo, John R. Ross, Louis Sass, Julia Stanley, Emily Stoper, Elizabeth Traugott, Monica Wilson, and Philip Zimbardo.

I should also like to thank the Center for Advanced Study for the Behavioral Sciences, where I was a Fellow in 1971–72 and where I did most of the research and writing underlying the first part of this book; and the National Science Foundation, which has supported the research for these studies under grant GS–38476.

PART I

Language
and Woman's Place

1 / Introduction

Language uses us as much as we use language. As much as our choice of forms of expression is guided by the thoughts we want to express, to the same extent the way we feel about the things in the real world governs the way we express ourselves about these things. Two words can be synonymous in their denotative sense, but one will be used in case a speaker feels favorably toward the object the word denotes, the other if he is unfavorably disposed. Similar situations are legion, involving unexpectedness, interest, and other emotional reactions on the part of the speaker to what he is talking about. Thus, while two speakers may be talking about the same thing or real-world situation, their descriptions may end up sounding utterly unrelated. The following well-known paradigm will be illustrative.

(1) *(a)* I am strong-minded.
   (b) You are obstinate.
   (c) He is pigheaded.

If it is indeed true that our feelings about the world color our expression of our thoughts, then we can use our linguistic behavior as a diagnostic of our hidden feelings about things. For often—as anyone with even a nodding acquaintance with modern psycho-analytic writing knows too well—we can interpret our overt actions, or our perceptions, in accordance with our desires, distorting them as we see fit. But the linguistic data are there, in black and white, or on tape, unambiguous and unavoidable. Hence, while in the ideal world other kinds of evidence for sociological phenomena would be desirable along with, or in addition to, linguistic evidence, sometimes at least the latter is all we can get with certainty. This is especially likely in emotionally charged areas like that of sexism and other forms of discriminatory behavior. This book, then, is an attempt to provide diagnostic evidence from language use for one type of inequity that has been claimed to exist in our society: that between the roles of men and women. I will attempt to discover what language use can tell us about the nature and extent of any inequity; and finally to ask whether anything can be done, from the linguistic end of the problem: does one correct a social inequity by changing linguistic disparities? We will find, I think, that women experience linguistic discrimination in two ways: in the way they are taught to use language, and in the way general language use treats them. Both tend, as we shall see, to rele-gate women to certain subservient functions: that of sex object, or servant; and therefore certain lexical items mean one thing applied to men, another to women, a difference that cannot be predicted except with reference to the different roles the sexes play in society.

The data on which I am basing my claims have been gathered mainly by introspection: I have examined my own speech and that of my acquaintances, and have used my own intuitions in analyzing it. I have also made use of the media: in some ways, the speech heard, for example, in commercials or situation comedies on television mir-rors the speech of the television-watching community: if it did not (not necessarily as an exact replica, but perhaps as a reflection of how the audience sees itself or wishes it were), it would not succeed. The sociologist, anthropologist or ethnomethodologist familar with what seem to him more error-proof data-gathering techniques, such as the recording of random conversation, may object that these introspective methods may produce dubious results. But first, it should be noted that *any* procedure is at some point introspective: the gatherer must analyze his data, after all. Then, one necessarily selects a subgroup of the population to work with: is the educated, white, middle-class group that the writer of the book identifies with less worthy of study than any other? And finally, there is the purely pragmatic issue: random conversation must go on for quite some time, and the recorder must be exceedingly lucky anyway, in order to produce evidence of any particular hypothesis, for example, that there is sexism in language, that there is not sexism in language. If we are to have a good sample of data to analyze, this will have to be elicited artificially from someone; I submit I am as good an artificial source of data as anyone.

These defenses are not meant to suggest that either the methodology or the results are final, or perfect. I mean to suggest one possible approach to the problem, one set of facts. I do feel that the majority of the claims I make will hold for the majority of speakers of English; that, in fact, much may, *mutatis mutandis,* be universal. But granting that this study does in itself represent the speech of only a small subpart of the community, it is still of use in indicating directions for further research in this area: in providing a basis for comparison, a taking-off point for further studies, a means of discovering what is universal in the data and what is not, and why. That is to say, I present what follows less as the final word on the subject of sexism in language —anything but that!—than as a goad to further research.

If a little girl "talks rough" like a boy, she will normally be ostracized, scolded, or made fun of. In this way society, in the form of a child's parents and friends, keeps her in line, in her place. This socializing process is, in most of its aspects, harmless and often necessary, but in this particular instance—the teaching of special linguistic uses to little girls—it raises serious problems, though the teachers may well be unaware of this. If the little girl learns her lesson well, she is not rewarded with unquestioned acceptance on the part of society; rather, the acquisition of this special style of speech will later be an excuse others use to keep her in a demeaning position, to refuse to take her seriously as a human being. Because of the way she speaks, the little girl—now grown to womanhood—will be accused of being unable to speak precisely or to express herself forcefully.

I am sure that the preceding paragraph contains an oversimplified description of the language-learning process in American society. Rather than saying that little boys and little girls, from the very start, learn two different ways of speaking, I think, from observation and reports by others, that the process is more complicated. Since the mother and other women are the dominant influences in the lives of most children under the age of five, probably both boys and girls first learn "women's language" as their first language. (I am told that in Japanese, children of both sexes use the particles proper for women until the age of five or so; then the little boy starts to be ridiculed if he uses them, and so soon learns to desist.) As they grow older, boys especially go through a stage of rough talk, as described by Spock and others; this is probably discouraged in little girls more strongly than in little boys, in whom parents may often find it more amusing than shocking. By the time children are ten or so, and split up into same-sex peer groups, the two languages are already present, according to my recollections and observations. But it seems that what has happened is that the boys have unlearned their original form of expression, and adopted new forms of expression, while the girls retain their old ways of speech. (One wonders whether this is related in any way to the often-noticed fact that little boys innovate, in their play, much more than little girls.) The ultimate result is the same, of course, whatever the interpretation.

So a girl is damned if she does, damned if she doesn't. If she refuses to talk like a lady, she is ridiculed and subjected to criticism as unfeminine; if she does learn, she is ridiculed as unable to think clearly, unable to take part in a serious discussion: in some sense, as less than fully human. These two choices which a woman has—to be less than a woman or less than a person—are highly painful.

An objection may be raised here that I am overstating the case against women's language, since most women who get as far as college learn to switch from women's to neutral language under appropriate situations (in class, talking to professors, at job interviews, and such). But I think this objection overlooks a number of problems. First, if a girl must learn two dialects, she becomes in effect a bilingual. Like many bilinguals, she may never really be master of either language, though her command of both is adequate enough for most purposes, she may never feel really comfortable using either, and never be certain that she is using the right one in the right place to the right person. Shifting from one language to another requires special awareness to the nuances of social situations, special alertness to possible disapproval. It may be that the extra energy that must be (subconsciously or otherwise) expended in this game is energy sapped from more creative work, and hinders women from expressing themselves as well, as fully, or as freely as they might otherwise. Thus, if a girl knows that a professor will be receptive to comments that sound scholarly, objective, unemotional, she will of course be tempted to use neutral language in class or in conference. But if she knows that, as a man, he will respond more approvingly to her at other levels if she uses women's language, and sounds frilly and feminine, won't she be confused as well as sorely tempted in two directions at once? It is often noticed that women participate less in class discussion than men— perhaps this linguistic indecisiveness is one reason why. (Incidentally, I don't find this true in my classes.)

It will be found that the overall effect of "women's language"— meaning both language restricted in use to women and language descriptive of women alone—is this: it submerges a woman's personal identity, by denying her the means of expressing herself strongly, on the one hand, and encouraging expressions that suggest triviality in subject matter and uncertainty about it; and, when a woman is being discussed, by treating her as an object—sexual or otherwise—but never a serious person with individual views. Of course, other forms of behavior in this society have the same purpose; but the phenomena seem especially clear linguistically.

The ultimate effect of these discrepancies is that women are systematically denied access to power, on the grounds that they are not capable of holding it as demonstrated by their linguistic behavior along with other aspects of their behavior; and the irony here is that women are made to feel that they deserve such treatment, because of inadequacies in their own intelligence and/or education. But in fact it is precisely because women have learned their lessons so well that they later suffer such discrimination. (This situation is of course true to some extent for all disadvantaged groups: white males of Anglo-Saxon descent set the standards and seem to expect other groups to be respectful of them but not to adopt them—they are to "keep in their place.")

I should like now to talk at length about some specific examples of linguistic phenomena I have described in general terms above. I want to talk first about the ways in which women's speech differs from men's speech; and then, to discuss a number of cases in which it seems clear that women are discriminated against (usually unconsciously) by the language everyone uses. I think it will become evident from this discussion that both types of phenomena reflect a deep bias on the part of our culture (and, indeed, of every culture I have ever heard of) against women being accorded full status as rational creatures and individuals in their own right; and finally, I would like to talk briefly about what might be done, and perhaps what should not be done, to remedy things.

2 / Talking Like a Lady

"Women's language" shows up in all levels of the grammar of English. We find differences in the choice and frequency of lexical items; in the situations in which certain syntactic rules are performed; in intonational and other supersegmental patterns. As an example of lexical differences, imagine a man and a woman both looking at the same wall, painted a pinkish shade of purple. The woman may say (2):

(2) The wall is mauve,

with no one consequently forming any special impression of her as a result of the words alone; but if the man should say (2), one might well conclude he was imitating a woman sarcastically or was a homosexual or an interior decorator. Women, then, make far more precise discriminations in naming colors than do men; words like *beige, ecru, aquamarine, lavender,* and so on are unremarkable in a woman's active vocabulary, but absent from that of most men. I have seen a man helpless with suppressed laughter at a discussion between two other people as to whether a book jacket was to be described as "lavender" or "mauve." Men find such discussion amusing because they consider such a question trivial, irrelevant to the real world.

We might ask why fine discrimination of color is relevant for women, but not for men. A clue is contained in the way many men in our society view other "unworldly" topics, such as high culture and the Church, as outside the world of men's work, relegated to women and men whose masculinity is not unquestionable. Men tend to relegate to women things that are not of concern to them, or do not involve their egos. Among these are problems of fine color discrimination. We might rephrase this point by saying that since women are not expected to make decisions on important matters, such as what kind of job to hold, they are relegated the noncrucial decisions as a sop. Deciding whether to name a color "lavender" or "mauve" is one such sop.

If it is agreed that this lexical disparity reflects a social inequity in the position of women, one may ask how to remedy it. Obviously, no one could seriously recommend legislating against the use of the terms "mauve" and "lavender" by women, or forcing men to learn to use them. All we can do is give women the opportunity to participate in the real decisions of life.

Aside from specific lexical items like color names, we find differences between the speech of women and that of men in the use of particles that grammarians often describe as "meaningless." There may be no referent for them, but they are far from meaningless: they define the social context of an utterance, indicate the relationship the speaker feels between himself and his addressee, between himself and what he is talking about.

As an experiment, one might present native speakers of standard American English with pairs of sentences, identical syntactically and in terms of referential lexical items, and differing merely in the choice of "meaningless" particle, and ask them which was spoken by a man, which a woman. Consider:

(3) *(a)* Oh dear, you've put the peanut butter in the refrigerator again.

   (b) Shit, you've put the peanut butter in the refrigerator again.

It is safe to predict that people would classify the first sentence as part of "women's language," the second as "men's language." It is true that many self-respecting women are becoming able to use sentences like (3) *(b)* publicly without flinching, but this is a relatively recent development, and while perhaps the majority of Middle America might condone the use of *(b)* for men, they would still disapprove of its use by women. (It is of interest, by the way, to note that men's language is increasingly being used by women, but women's language is not being adopted by men, apart from those who reject the American masculine image [for example, homosexuals]. This is analogous to the fact that men's jobs are being sought by women, but few men are rushing to become housewives or secretaries. The language of the favored group, the group that holds the power, along with its nonlinguistic behavior, is generally adopted by the other group, not vice versa. In any event, it is a truism to state that the "stronger" expletives are reserved for men, and the "weaker" ones for women.)

Now we may ask what we mean by "stronger" and "weaker" expletives. (If these particles were indeed meaningless, none would be stronger than any other.) The difference between using "shit" (or "damn," or one of many others) as opposed to "oh dear," or "goodness," or "oh fudge" lies in how forcefully one says how one feels—perhaps, one might say, choice of particle is a function of how strongly one allows oneself to feel about something, so that the strength of an emotion conveyed in a sentence corresponds to the strength of the particle. Hence in a really serious situation, the use of "trivializing" (that is, "women's") particles constitutes a joke, or at any rate, is highly inappropriate. (In conformity with current linguistic practice, throughout this work an asterisk (*) will be used to mark a sentence that is inappropriate in some sense, either because it is syntactically deviant or used in the wrong social context.)

(4) *(a)* *Oh fudge, my hair is on fire.

   (b) *Dear me, did he kidnap the baby?

As children, women are encouraged to be "little ladies." Little ladies don't scream as vociferously as little boys, and they are chastised more severely for throwing tantrums or showing temper: "high spirits" are expected and therefore tolerated in little boys; docility and resignation are the corresponding traits expected of little girls. Now, we tend to excuse a show of temper by a man where we would not excuse an identical tirade from a woman: women are allowed to fuss and complain, but only a man can bellow in rage. It is sometimes claimed that there is a biological basis for this behavior difference, though I don't believe conclusive evidence exists that the early differences in behavior that have been observed are not the results of very different treatment of babies of the two sexes from the beginning; but surely the use of different particles by men and women is a learned trait, merely mirroring nonlinguistic differences again, and again pointing out an inequity that exists between the treatment of men, and society's expectations of them, and the treatment of women. Allowing men stronger means of expression than are open to women further reinforces men's position of strength in the real world: for surely we listen with more attention the more strongly and forcefully someone expresses opinions, and a speaker unable—for whatever reason—to be forceful in stating his views is much less likely to be taken seriously. Ability to use strong particles like "shit" and "hell" is, of course, only incidental to the inequity that exists rather than its cause. But once again, apparently accidental linguistic usage suggests that women are denied equality partially for linguistic reasons, and that an examination of language points up precisely an area in which inequity exists. Further, if someone is allowed to show emotions, and consequently does, others may well be able to view him as a real individual in his own right, as they could not if he never showed emotion. Here again, then, the behavior a woman learns as "correct" prevents her from being taken seriously as an individual, and further is considered "correct" and necessary for a woman precisely because society does *not* consider her seriously as an individual.

Similar sorts of disparities exist elsewhere in the vocabulary. There is, for instance, a group of adjectives which have, besides their specific and literal meanings, another use, that of indicating the speaker's approbation or admiration for something. Some of these adjectives are neutral as to sex of speaker: either men or women may use them. But another set seems, in its figurative use, to be largely confined to women's speech. Representative lists of both types are below:

neutral	*women only*
great	adorable
terrific	charming
cool	sweet
neat	lovely
	divine

As with the color words and swear words already discussed, for a man to stray into the "women's" column is apt to be damaging to his reputation, though here a woman may freely use the neutral words. But it should not be inferred from this that a woman's use of the "women's" words is without its risks. Where a woman has a choice between the neutral words and the women's words, as a man has not, she may be suggesting very different things about her own personality and her view of the subject matter by her choice of words of the first set or words of the second.

(5) *(a)* What a terrific idea!
   (b) What a divine idea!

It seems to me that *(a)* might be used under any appropriate conditions by a female speaker. But *(b)* is more restricted. Probably it is used appropriately (even by the sort of speaker for whom it was normal) only in case the speaker feels the idea referred to to be essentially frivolous, trivial, or unimportant to the world at large—only an amusement for the speaker herself. Consider, then, a woman advertising executive at an advertising conference. However feminine an advertising executive she is, she is much more likely to express her approval with (5) *(a)* than with *(b),* which might cause raised eyebrows, and the reaction: "That's what we get for putting a woman in charge of this company."

On the other hand, suppose a friend suggests to the same woman that she should dye her French poodles to match her cigarette lighter.

In this case, the suggestion really concerns only her, and the impression she will make on people. In this case, she may use *(b)*, from the "woman's language." So the choice is not really free: words restricted to "women's language" suggest that concepts to which they are applied are not relevant to the real world of (male) influence and power.

One may ask whether there really are no analogous terms that are available to men—terms that denote approval of the trivial, the personal; that express approbation in terms of one's own personal emotional reaction, rather than by gauging the likely general reaction. There does in fact seem to be one such word: it is the hippie invention "groovy," which seems to have most of the connotations that separate "lovely" and "divine" from "great" and "terrific" excepting only that it does not mark the speaker as feminine or effeminate.

(6) *(a)* What a terrific steel mill!
   (b) *What a lovely steel mill! (male speaking)
   (c) What a groovy steel mill!

I think it is significant that this word was introduced by the hippies, and, when used seriously rather than sarcastically, used principally by people who have accepted the hippies' values. Principal among these is the denial of the Protestant work ethic: to a hippie, something can be worth thinking about even if it isn't influential in the power structure, or moneymaking. Hippies are separated from the activities of the real world just as women are—though in the former case it is due to a decision on their parts, while this is not uncontroversially true in the case of women. For both these groups, it is possible to express approval of things in a personal way—though one does so at the risk of losing one's credibility with members of the power structure. It is also true, according to some speakers, that upper-class British men may use the words listed in the "women's" column, as well as the specific color words and others we have categorized as specifically feminine, without raising doubts as to their masculinity among other speakers of the same dialect. (This is not true for lower-class Britons, however.) The reason may be that commitment to the work ethic need not necessarily be displayed: one may be or appear to be a gentleman of leisure, interested in various pursuits, but not involved in mundane (business or political) affairs, in such a culture, without incurring disgrace. This is rather analogous to the position of a woman in American middle-class society, so we should not be surprised if these special lexical items are usable by both groups. This fact points indeed to a more general conclusion. These words aren't, basically, "feminine"; rather, they signal "uninvolved," or "out of power." Any group in a society to which these labels are applicable may presumably use these words; they are often considered "feminine," "unmasculine," because women are the "uninvolved," "out of power" group *par excellence*.

Another group that has, ostensibly at least, taken itself out of the search for power and money is that of academic men. They are frequently viewed by other groups as analogous in some ways to women—they don't really work, they are supported in their frivolous pursuits by others, what they do doesn't really count in the real world, and so on. The suburban home finds its counterpart in the ivory tower: one is supposedly shielded from harsh realities in both. Therefore it is not too surprising that many academic men (especially those who emulate British norms) may violate many of these sacrosanct rules I have just laid down: they often use "women's language." Among themselves, this does not occasion ridicule. But to a truck driver, a professor saying, "What a lovely hat!" is undoubtedly laughable, all the more so as it reinforces his stereotype of professors as effete snobs.

When we leave the lexicon and venture into syntax, we find that syntactically too women's speech is peculiar. To my knowledge, there is no syntactic rule in English that only women may use. But there is at least one rule that a woman will use in more conversational situations than a man. (This fact indicates, of course, that the applicability of syntactic rules is governed partly by social context—the positions in society of the speaker and addressee, with respect to each other, and the impression one seeks to make on the other.) This is the rule of tag-question formation.[1]

1. Within the lexicon itself, there seems to be a parallel phenomenon to tag-question usage, which I refrain from discussing in the body of the text because the facts are controversial and I do not understand them fully. The intensive *so,* used where purists would insist upon an absolute superlative, heavily stressed, seems more characteristic of women's language than of men's, though it is found in the latter, particularly in the

A tag, in its usage as well as its syntactic shape (in English) is midway between an outright statement and a yes-no question: it is less assertive than the former, but more confident than the latter. Therefore it is usable under certain contextual situations: not those in which a statement would be appropriate, nor those in which a yes-no question is generally used, but in situations intermediate between these.

One makes a statement when one has confidence in his knowledge and is pretty certain that his statement will be believed; one asks a question when one lacks knowledge on some point and has reason to believe that this gap can and will be remedied by an answer by the addressee. A tag question, being intermediate between these, is used when the speaker is stating a claim, but lacks full confidence in the truth of that claim. So if I say

(7) Is John here?

I will probably not be surprised if my respondent answers "no"; but if I say

(8) John is here, isn't he?

instead, chances are I am already biased in favor of a positive answer, wanting only confirmation by the addressee. I still want a response from him, as I do with a yes-no question; but I have enough knowledge (or think I have) to predict that response, much as with a

---

speech of male academics. Consider, for instance, the following sentences:

(a) I feel *so* unhappy! .
(b) That movie made me *so* sick!

Men seem to have the least difficulty using this construction when the sentence is unemotional, or nonsubjective—without reference to the speaker himself:

(c) That sunset is *so* beautiful!
(d) Fred is *so* dumb!

Substituting an equative like *so* for absolute superlatives (like *very, really, utterly*) seems to be a way of backing out of committing oneself strongly to an opinion, rather like tag questions (cf. discussion below, in the text). One might hedge in this way with perfect right in making aesthetic judgments, as in *(c)*, or intellectual judgments, as in *(d)*. But it is somewhat odd to hedge in describing one's own mental or emotional state: who, after all, is qualified to contradict one on this? To hedge in this situation is to seek to avoid making any strong statement: a characteristic, as we have noted already and shall note further, of women's speech.

declarative statement. A tag question, then, might be thought of as a declarative statement without the assumption that the statement is to be believed by the addressee: one has an out, as with a question. A tag gives the addressee leeway, not forcing him to go along with the views of the speaker.

There are situations in which a tag is legitimate, in fact the only legitimate sentence form. So, for example, if I have seen something only indistinctly, and have reason to believe my addressee had a better view, I can say:

(9) I had my glasses off. He was out at third, wasn't he?

Sometimes we find a tag question used in cases in which the speaker knows as well as the addressee what the answer must be, and doesn't need confirmation. One such situation is when the speaker is making "small talk," trying to elicit conversation from the addressee:

(10) Sure is hot here, isn't it?

In discussing personal feelings or opinions, only the speaker normally has any way of knowing the correct answer. Strictly speaking, questioning one's own opinions is futile. Sentences like (11) are usually ridiculous.

(11) *I have a headache, don't I?

But similar cases do, apparently, exist, in which it is the speaker's opinions, rather than perceptions, for which corroboration is sought, as in (12):

(12) The way prices are rising is horrendous, isn't it?

While there are of course other possible interpretations of a sentence like this, one possibility is that the speaker has a particular answer in mind—"yes" or "no"—but is reluctant to state it baldly. It is my impression, though I do not have precise statistical evidence, that this sort of tag question is much more apt to be used by women than by men. If this is indeed true, why is it true?

These sentence types provide a means whereby a speaker can avoid committing himself, and thereby avoid coming into conflict with the addressee. The problem is that, by so doing, a speaker may also give the impression of not being really sure of himself, of looking to the addressee for confirmation, even of having no views of his own. This last criticism is, of course, one often leveled at women. One wonders how much of it reflects a use of language that has been imposed on women from their earliest years.

Related to this special use of a syntactic rule is a widespread difference perceptible in women's intonational patterns.[2] There is a peculiar sentence intonation pattern, found in English as far as I know only among women, which has the form of a declarative answer to a question, and is used as such, but has the rising inflection typical of a yes-no question, as well as being especially hesitant. The effect is as though one were seeking confirmation, though at the same time the speaker may be the only one who has the requisite information.

(13) *(a)* When will dinner be ready?
    (b) Oh . . . around six o'clock . . . ?

It is as though *(b)* were saying, "Six o'clock, if that's OK with you, if you agree." *(a)* is put in the position of having to provide confirmation, and *(b)* sounds unsure. Here we find unwillingness to assert an opinion carried to an extreme. One likely consequence is that these sorts of speech patterns are taken to reflect something real about character and play a part in not taking a woman seriously or trusting her with any real responsibilities, since "she can't make up her mind" and "isn't sure of herself." And here again we see that people form judgments about other people on the basis of superficial linguistic behavior that may have nothing to do with inner character, but has been imposed upon the speaker, on pain of worse punishment than not being taken seriously.

Such features are probably part of the general fact that women's

2. For analogues outside of English to these uses of tag questions and special intonation patterns, ct. my discussion of Japanese particles in "Language in Context," *Language,* 48 (1972), 907–27. It is to be expected that similar cases will be found in many other languages as well. See, for example, M. R. Haas's very interesting discussion of differences between men's and women's speech (mostly involving lexical dissimilarities) in many languages, in D. Hymes, ed., *Language in Culture and Society* (New York: Harper & Row, 1964).

speech sounds much more "polite" than men's. One aspect of politeness is as we have just described: leaving a decision open, not imposing your mind, or views, or claims on anyone else. Thus a tag question is a kind of polite statement, in that it does not force agreement or belief on the addressee. A request may be in the same sense a polite command, in that it does not overtly require obedience, but rather suggests something be done as a favor to the speaker. An overt order (as in an imperative) expresses the (often impolite) assumption of the speaker's superior position to the addressee, carrying with it the right to enforce compliance, whereas with a request the decision on the face of it is left up to the addressee. (The same is true of suggestions: here, the implication is not that the addressee is in danger if he does not comply—merely that he will be glad if he does. Once again, the decision is up to the addressee, and a suggestion therefore is politer than an order.) The more particles in a sentence that reinforce the notion that it is a request, rather than an order, the politer the result. The sentences of (14) illustrate these points: (14) *(a)* is a direct order, *(b)* and *(c)* simple requests, and *(d)* and *(e)* compound requests.[3]

(14) *(a)* Close the door.
    (b) Please close the door.
    (c) Will you close the door?
    (d) Will you please close the door?
    (e) Won't you close the door?

Let me first explain why *(e)* has been classified as a compound request. (A sentence like *Won't you please close the door* would then count as a doubly compound request.) A sentence like (14) *(c)* is close in sense to "Are you willing to close the door?" According to the normal rules of polite conversation, to agree that you are willing is to agree to do the thing asked of you. Hence this apparent inquiry functions as a request, leaving the decision up to the willingness of the addressee. Phrasing it as a positive question makes the (implicit) assumption that a "yes" answer will be forthcoming. Sentence (14) *(d)* is more polite than *(b)* or *(c)* because it combines them: *please*

3. For more detailed discussion of these problems, see Lakoff, "Language in Context."

indicating that to accede will be to do something for the speaker, and *will you,* as noted, suggesting that the addressee has the final decision. If, now, the question is phrased with a negative, as in (14) *(e),* the speaker seems to suggest the stronger likelihood of a negative response from the addressee. Since the assumption is then that the addressee is that much freer to refuse, (14) *(e)* acts as a more polite request than (14) *(c)* or *(d): (c)* and *(d)* put the burden of refusal on the addressee, as *(e)* does not.

Given these facts, one can see the connection between tag questions and tag orders and other requests. In all these cases, the speaker is not committed as with a simple declarative or affirmative. And the more one compounds a request, the more characteristic it is of women's speech, the less of men's. A sentence that begins *Won't you please* (without special emphasis on *please*) seems to me at least to have a distinctly unmasculine sound. Little girls are indeed taught to talk like little ladies, in that their speech is in many ways more polite than that of boys or men, and the reason for this is that politeness involves an absence of a strong statement, and women's speech is devised to prevent the expression of strong statements.

3 / Talking about Women

We have thus far confined ourselves to one facet of the problem of women and the English language: the way in which women prejudice the case against themselves by their use of language. But it is at least as true that others—as well as women themselves—make matters so by the way in which they refer to women. Often a word that may be used of both men and women (and perhaps of things as well), when applied to women, assumes a special meaning that, by implication rather than outright assertion, is derogatory to women as a group.

When a word acquires a bad connotation by association with something unpleasant or embarrassing, people may search for substitutes that do not have the uncomfortable effect—that is, euphemisms. Since attitudes toward the original referent are not altered by a change of name, the new name itself takes on the adverse connotations, and a new euphemism must be found. It is no doubt possible to pick out areas of particular psychological strain or discomfort—areas where problems exist in a culture—by pinpointing items around which a great many euphemisms are clustered. An obvious example concerns the various words for that household convenience into which human wastes are eliminated: toilet, bathroom, rest room, comfort station, lavatory, water closet, loo, and all the others.

In the case of women, it may be encouraging to find no richness of euphemism; but it is discouraging to note that at least one euphemism for "woman" does exist and is very much alive. The word, of course, is "lady," which seems to be replacing "woman" in a great many contexts. Where both exist, they have different connotations; where only one exists, there is usually a reason, to be found in the context in which the word is uttered.

Related to the existence of euphemistic terms for "woman" is the existence of euphemistic terms for woman's principal role, that of "housewife." Most occupational terms do not have coexisting euphemisms: these seem to come into being only when the occupation is considered embarrassing or demeaning. Thus there is no euphemism for "professor," "doctor," "bank president"; but we do find "mortician" and "funeral director" for "undertaker"; "custodian" and "sanitary engineer" for "janitor"; "domestic" for "cleaning woman"; and so forth. Similarly one keeps running into hopeful suggestions, principally in the pages of women's magazines, that the lot of the housewife would be immeasurably improved if she thought of herself as "homemaker," "household executive," "household engineer," or any of several others. I am not sure what to make of the fact that none of these (unlike those of the bona fide occupational euphemisms) have taken hold: is it because the "housewife" doesn't consider her status demeaning? Then why the search for euphemisms? Or does she feel that there is no escape through a change in nomenclature, or lack pride in her job to such an extent that she doesn't feel up to making the effort? This is a question for the sociologist.

It may be objected that *lady* has a masculine counterpart, namely *gentleman,* occasionally shortened to *gent.* But I don't think this is a fair comparison. *Lady* is much more common than *gent(leman),* and, since *gent* exists, the reason is not ease of pronunciation. *Lady* is really a euphemism for *woman,* but *gentleman* is not nearly frequent enough to classify as a euphemism for *man.* Just as we do not call whites "Caucasian-Americans," there is no felt need to refer to men commonly as "gentlemen." And just as there is a need for such terms as "Afro-Americans," there is similarly a felt need for "lady." One might even say that when a derogatory epithet exists, a parallel euphemism is deemed necessary. (The term WASP, white Anglo-Saxon Protestant, may occur to the reader as a possible derogatory term which has no parallel euphemism. But in fact, WASP is not parallel in usage to *nigger, polack,* or *yid.* One can refer to himself as a WASP, as one cannot refer to himself as a *nigger* without either a total lack of self-pride or bitter sarcasm. Thus one can say: "Sure I'm a WASP, and proud of it!" but probably not: "Sure I'm a nigger, and proud of it!" without special sarcastic inflection in the voice suggesting that it is an imitation of the addressee.) To avoid having to resort to terms like "Afro-American," we need only get rid of all expressions like "nigger"; to banish "lady" in its euphemistic sense from the vocabulary of English, we need only first get rid of "broad" and its relations. But of course, as already pointed out, we cannot achieve this commendable simplification of the lexicon unless we somehow remove from our minds the idea that blacks *are* niggers, and that women *are* broads. The presence of the words is a signal that something is wrong, rather than (as too often interpreted by well-meaning reformers) the problem itself. The point here is that, unless we start feeling more respect for women and, at the same time, less uncomfortable about them and their roles in society in relation to men, we cannot avoid *ladies* any more than we can avoid *broads.*

In the past, some ethnic groups that today are relatively respectable were apparently considered less so. And in looking at reports of the terms used to describe those groups at the earlier time, we find two interesting facts: first, there is a much greater incidence of derogatory epithets for that group (as might be expected); and second (which one might not be led to expect automatically) there exist euphemistic terms for that group that are no longer in general use. One can only conclude that euphemisms vanish as they are no longer needed. The example I have in mind is that of the words used to describe Jews. Aside from the uncomplimentary epithets which still exist today, though not encountered very often, one finds, in reading novels written and set more than half a century ago, a number of euphemisms that are not found any more, such as "Hebrew gentleman" and "Israelite." The disappearance of the euphemisms concurrently with the derogatory terms suggests that women will be *ladies* until some more dignified status can be found for them.

It might also be claimed that *lady* is no euphemism because it has exactly the same connotations as woman, is usable under the same semantic and contextual conditions. But a cursory inspection will show that this is not always the case. The decision to use one term rather than the other may considerably alter the sense of a sentence. The following are examples:

(15) *(a)* A (woman) that I know makes amazing things out of
    (lady)

    shoelaces and old boxes.

(b) A (woman) I know works at Woolworth's.
    (lady)

(c) A (woman) I know is a dean at Berkeley.
    (lady)

(These facts are true for some speakers of English. For others, *lady* has taken over the function of *woman* to such an extent that *lady* can be used in all these sentences.)

In my speech, the use of *lady* in (15) *(c)* imparts a frivolous or nonserious tone to the sentence: the matter under discussion is one of not too great moment. In this dialect, then, *lady* seems to be the more colloquial word: it is less apt to be used in writing, or in discussing serious matters. Similarly in (15) *(a)*, using *lady* would suggest that the speaker considered the "amazing things" not to be serious art, but merely a hobby or an aberration. If *woman* is used, she might be a serious (pop art) sculptor.

Related to this is the use of *lady* in job terminology. For at least some speakers, the more demeaning the job, the more the person holding it (if female, of course) is likely to be described as a *lady*. Thus, *cleaning lady* is at least as common as *cleaning woman, saleslady* as *saleswoman*. But one says, normally, *woman doctor*. To say *lady doctor* is to be very condescending: it constitutes an insult. For men, there is no such dichotomy. *Garbageman* or *salesman* is the only possibility, never **garbage gentleman*. And of course, since in the professions the male is unmarked, we never have **man (male) doctor*.

Numerous other examples can be given, all tending to prove the same point: that if, in a particular sentence, both *woman* and *lady* might be used, the use of the latter tends to trivialize the subject matter under discussion, often subtly ridiculing the woman involved. Thus, for example, a mention in the San Francisco *Chronicle* of January 31, 1972, of Madalyn Murray O'Hair as the "lady atheist" reduces her position to that of scatterbrained eccentric, or at any rate, one who need not be taken seriously. Even *woman atheist* is scarcely defensible: first, because her sex is irrelevant to her philosophical position, and second, because her name makes it clear in any event. But *lady* makes matters still worse. Similarly a reference to a *woman sculptor* is only mildly annoying (since there is no term **male sculptor*, the discrepancy suggests that such activity is normal for a man, but not for a woman), but still it could be used with reference to a serious artist. *Lady sculptor*, on the other hand, strikes me as a slur against the artist, deliberate or not, implying that the woman's art is frivolous, something she does to fend off the boredom of suburban housewifery, or at any rate, nothing of moment in the art world. Serious artists have shows, not *dilettantes*. So we hear of *one-woman shows*, but never *one-lady shows*.

Another realm of usage in which *lady* contrasts with *woman* is in titles of organizations. It seems that organizations of women who have a serious purpose (not merely that of spending time with one another) cannot use the word *lady* in their titles, but less serious ones may. Compare the *Ladies' Auxiliary* of a men's group, or the *Thursday Evening Ladies Browning and Garden Society* with **Ladies' Lib* or **Ladies Strike for Peace*.

What is curious about this split is that *lady* is, as noted, in origin a euphemism for *woman*. What kind of euphemism is it that subtly denigrates the people to whom it refers, suggests that they are not to be taken seriously, are laughing stocks? A euphemism, after all, is supposed to put a better face on something people find uncomfortable. But this is not really contradictory. What a euphemism is supposed to do, actually, is to remove from thought *that part* of the connotations of a word that creates the discomfort. So each of the euphemisms for toilet, starting with *toilet,* seems to be trying to get further from the notion of excrement, by employing successively more elegant terminology that seems designed to suggest that the piece of furniture in question has really other primary uses, for performing one's toilette, for washing, for comfort, for resting, but never for those other things. Perhaps the notion of the nonseriousness of women is not the thing that makes men—the devisers of euphemism—as well as women, uncomfortable. Perhaps it is some other aspect of the man-woman relationship. How can we determine whether this is in fact the case?

One way of identifying the precise source of discomfort is, perhaps, by looking at the derogatory terms for something. Many of the terms for blacks refer to their physical characteristics. And the latest euphemism for blacks, *Afro-Americans,* seems to be a specific attempt to get away from color names. (The term *black* is not a euphemism, but rather an attempt to confront the issue squarely and make color into a source of pride.) And as has often been noted, derogatory terms for women are very often overtly sexual: the reader will have no difficulty recalling what I allude to here.

The distinction between *lady* and *woman,* in those dialects of American English in which it is found, may be traceable to other causes than the sexual connotations present in *woman.* Most people who are asked why they have chosen to use *lady* where *woman* would be as appropriate will reply that *lady* seemed more polite. The concept of politeness thus invoked is the politeness used in dignifying or ennobling a concept that normally is not thought of as having dignity or nobility. It is this notion of politeness that explains why we have *cleaning lady,* but not, normally, *lady doctor.* A doctor does not need to be exalted by conventional expressions: she has dignity enough from her professional status. But a cleaning woman is in a very different situation, in which her occupational category requires ennobling. Then perhaps we can say that the very notion of womanhood, as opposed to manhood, requires ennobling since it lacks inherent dignity of its own: hence the word *woman* requires the existence of a euphemism like *lady*. Besides or possibly because of being explicitly devoid of sexual connotation, *lady* carries with it overtones recalling the age of chivalry: the exalted stature of the person so referred to, her existence above the common sphere. This makes the term seem polite at first, but we must also remember that these implications are perilous: they suggest that a "lady" is helpless, and cannot do things for herself. In this respect the use of a word like *lady* is parallel to the act of opening doors for women—or ladies. At first blush it is flattering: the object of the flattery feels honored, cherished, and so forth; but by the same token, she is also considered helpless and not in control of her own destiny. Women who protest that they *like* receiving these little courtesies, and object to being liberated from them, should reflect a bit on their deeper meaning and see how much they like *that*.

This brings us to the consideration of another common substitute for *woman*, namely *girl*. One seldom hears a man past the age of adolescence referred to as a boy, save in expressions like "going out with the boys," which are meant to suggest an air of adolescent frivolity and irresponsibility. But women of all ages are "girls": one can have a man, not a boy, Friday, but a girl, never a woman or even a lady, Friday; women have girl friends, but men do not—in a nonsexual sense—have boyfriends. It may be that this use of *girl* is euphemistic in the sense in which *lady* is a euphemism: in stressing the idea of immaturity, it removes the sexual connotations lurking in *woman*. Instead of the ennobling present in *lady, girl* is (presumably) flattering to women because of its stress on youth. But here again there are pitfalls: in recalling youth, frivolity, and immaturity, *girl* brings to mind irresponsibility: you don't send a girl to do a woman's errand (or even, for that matter, a boy's errand). It seems that again, by an appeal to feminine vanity (about which we shall have more to say later) the users of English have assigned women to a very unflattering place in their minds: a woman is a person who is both too immature and too far from real life to be entrusted with responsibilities and with decisions of any serious nature. Would you elect president a person incapable of putting on her own coat? (Of course, if we were to have a married woman president, we would not have any name for her husband parallel to *First Lady,* and why do you suppose that is?)

Perhaps the way in which *lady* functions as a euphemism for *woman* is that it does not contain the sexual implications present in *woman:* it is not "embarrassing" in that way. If this is so, we may expect that, in the future, *lady* will replace *woman* as the primary word for the human female, since *woman* will have become too blatantly sexual. That this distinction is already made in some contexts at least is shown in the following examples:

(16) *(a)* She's only twelve, but she's already a woman.
                            *lady
    (b) After ten years in jail, Harry wanted to find a woman.
                                      *lady
    (c) She's my woman, see, so don't mess around with her.
    *lady

It may be, finally, that the reason the use of *lady* rather than *woman* in a sentence creates the impression of frivolity discussed above precisely because of the euphemistic nature of *lady.* In serious discussion, one does not typically employ euphemisms. So, for instance, a sentence like (17)*(a)* is more suited to cocktail party chitchat by returning tourists than to learned discussion by anthropologists, who would be more likely to use a technical term, as in (17)*(b)*:

(17) *(a)* When the natives of Mbanga want to use the little boys' room, first they find a large pineapple leaf. . . .
    (b) When the natives of Mbanga wish to defecate, first they find a large pineapple leaf. . . .

Perhaps the discomfort men suffer in contemplating, more or less unconsciously, the sexuality of women is traceable to guilt feelings on their part. The guilt arises, I should think, not only because they think sex is inherently dirty (that is another problem) but because if one deals with women as primarily sexual beings, one is in effect automatically relegating them to object status; if women are there for the use and enjoyment of men, they are not fully human beings in their own right. But women are in most other respects evidently human. So a man feels somewhat ambivalent—more or less consciously—and reacts all the more strongly for that reason. Hence, perhaps, the rather hysterical ridicule heaped on Women's Lib in the media. In any case, throughout English one finds evidence of many sorts that women are viewed (by women as well as men) as secondary beings: as having an existence only when defined by a man.

These facts about women's position should cause us to question one of the commonest criticisms made of women's behavior, as opposed to men's: one often hears that women are vain and self-centered, concerned only about their appearance and how others view them. A little thought should convince anyone that, in fact, it is men who are self-centered and egocentric and that women's seeming vanity is not that at all.

As noted above, a woman's reputation and position in society depend almost wholly on the impression she makes upon others, how others view her. She must dress decoratively, look attractive, be compliant, if she is to survive at all in the world. Then her overattention to appearance and appearances (including, perhaps overcorrectness and overgentility of speech and etiquette) is merely the result of being forced to exist only as a reflection in the eyes of others. She does not, cannot, do anything in her own behalf or purely for her own pleasure or aggrandizement. (Rather ironically, the only way she can increase her own comfort, pleasure, and security is through her husband's advancement, and thus she can achieve material comforts only through someone else's efforts. What seem to be self-centered efforts are really aimed at the opinions of others, and what appear to be efforts for someone else are really the only ones permissible for a woman's own behalf. It is no wonder women lack an identity and feel they have no place of their own.)

In fact, men are the vain sex. Men may derive pleasure directly from their own works. Men do things purely for their own satisfaction, not caring nearly so much how it will look to others. This, surely, is the true egocentricity. Further, it seems to me that the ultimate vanity or self-centeredness is to be found in eccentricity. The eccentric alone truly cares only for himself and his own pleasure: he does not concern himself with how his actions affect others or look to others. And eccentricity is far more common and far more tolerated in men than in women. A strong personality in general, a mark of egocentricity, is again valued in men much more than in women. For these reasons, women are not very successful in business or politics, where both vanity and eccentricity of certain sorts can be marks of distinction rather than objects of ridicule.

Sociologically it is probably fairly obvious that a woman in most subcultures in our society achieves status only through her father's, husband's, or lover's position. What is remarkable is that these facts show up linguistically in nonobvious ways.

Suppose we take a pair of words which, in terms of the possible relationships in an earlier society, were simple male-female equivalents, analogous to bull: cow. Suppose we find that, for independent reasons, society has changed in such a way that the primary meanings now are irrelevant. Yet the words have not been discarded, but have acquired new meanings, metaphorically related to their original senses. But suppose these new metaphorical uses are no longer parallel to each other. By seeing where the parallelism breaks down, we can intuit something about the different roles played by men and women in this culture. One good example of such a divergence through time is found in the pair *master* and *mistress*. Once used with reference to one person's power over another, these words became unusable in their original sense as the master-servant relationship became nonexistent. But the words are still common as used in sentences (18) and (19):

(18) *(a)* He is a master of the intricacies of academic politics.
     (b) *She is a mistress . . .

(19) *(a)* *Harry declined to be my master, and so returned to his wife.
     (b) Rhonda declined to be my mistress, and so returned to her husband.

Unless used with reference to animals or slaves, *master* now generally refers to a man who has acquired consummate ability in some field, normally nonsexual. But its feminine counterpart cannot be used in this way. It is practically restricted to its sexual sense of "paramour." We start out with two terms, both roughly paraphrasable as "one who has power over another." But the masculine form, once one person is no longer able to have absolute power over another, becomes usable metaphorically in the sense of "have power over *something.*" The feminine counterpart also acquired a metaphorical interpretation, but the metaphor here is sexual: one's mistress "has power over" one in a sexual sense. And this expression is probably chivalrous, rather than descriptive of the real-world relationship between lovers. In terms of choice, of economic control, and so forth, it is generally the man who holds the power in such a relationship; to call a woman one's "mistress" is the equivalent of saying "please" in prefacing a request to a subordinate. Both are done for politeness and are done purely because both participants in the relationship, in both cases, know that the supposed inferiority of the mistress's lover and of the user of "please" is only a sham. Interesting too in this regard is the fact that "master" requires as its object only the name of some activity, something inanimate and abstract. But "mistress" requires a masculine noun in the possessive to precede it. One cannot say:

(20) *Rhonda is a mistress.

One must be *someone's* mistress.

And obviously too, it is one thing to be an *old master,* like Hans Holbein, and another to be an *old mistress:* the latter, again, requires a masculine possessive form preceding it, indicating who has done the discarding. *Old* in the first instance refers to absolute age: the artist's lifetime versus the time of writing. But *old* in the second really means "discarded," "old" with respect to someone else.

Others, too, have been struck by the hidden assumptions in the word *mistress.* In an article on the Op-Ed page of the *New York Times,* July 20, 1972, Rebecca Reyher suggests that a way around this difficulty is to adopt a parallel term for the man in such a relationship: stud. But further thought will make it clear that the use of this new term will not obviate the problem: the roots lie deeper, in the social nature of the relationship itself. As long as it is the woman who is dependent on the man, socially and economically, in such relationships, there will be no possibility of coining a parallel term for *mistress*. Just as we will have the sorts of disparities illustrated by sentences (18)–(19), we will find further disparities, for the same reasons. Note, for instance, the difference in the acceptability of: He's a real stud! as contrasted to: *She's a real mistress!

So here we see several important points concerning the relationship between men and women illustrated: first, that men are defined in terms of what they do in the world, women in terms of the men with whom they are associated; and second, that the notion of "power" for a man is different from that of "power" for a woman: it is acquired and manifested in different ways. One might say then that these words have retained their principal meanings through time; what has changed is the kinds of interpersonal relationships to which they refer.

As a second example, the examples in (21) should be completely parallel semantically:

(21) *(a)* He's a professional.
     (b) She's a professional.

Hearing and knowing no more about the subjects of the discourse than this, what would one assume about them in each case? Certainly in *(a)* the normal conclusion the casual eavesdropper would come to was that "he" was a doctor or a lawyer or a member of one of the other professions. But it is much less likely that one would draw a similar conclusion in *(b)*. Rather, the first assumption most speakers of English seem to make is that "she" is a prostitute, literally or figuratively speaking. Again, a man is defined in the serious world by what he does, a woman by her sexuality, that is, in terms of one particular aspect of her relationship to men.

This discrepancy is not confined to English. Victor Wen has informed me that a similar situation pertains in Chinese. One may say of a man, "He's in business," and of a woman, "She's in business," lexically and grammatically parallel. The former means about what its English equivalent means. But the latter is synonymous to sentence (21) *(b)*.

James Fox tells me that in many cultures, as in English, people may be referred to metaphorically by animal names, suggesting that they have some of the attributes of that animal, real or part of the folklore. What is interesting here is that where animal names may be applied to both men and women—whether or not there are separate terms for male and female in the animal—the former may have connotations in all sorts of areas, while the latter, whatever other connotations the term may suggest, nearly always makes sexual reference as well. Compare in this regard *dog* and *bitch, fox* and *vixen,* and the difference between *he's a pig* and *she's a pig.*

The sexual definition of women, however, is but one facet of a much larger problem. In every aspect of life, a woman is identified in terms of the men she relates to. The opposite is not usually true of men: they act in the world as autonomous individuals, but women are only "John's wife," or "Harry's girl friend." Thus, meeting a woman at a party, a quite normal opening conversational gambit might be: "What does your husband do?" One very seldom hears, in a similar situation, a question addressed to a man: "What does your wife do?" The question would, to a majority of men, seem tautological: "She's my wife—that's what she does." This is true even in cases in which a woman is being discussed in a context utterly unrelated to her relationships with men, when she has attained sufficient stature to be considered for high public office. In fact, in a recent discussion of possible Supreme Court nominees, one woman was mentioned prominently. In discussing her general qualifications for the office, and her background, the *New York Times* saw fit to remark on her "bathing-beauty figure." Note that this is not only a judgment on a physical attribute totally removed from her qualifications for the Supreme Court, but that it is couched in terms of how a man would react to her figure. Some days later, President Nixon announced the nominations to his Price Board, among them one woman. In the thumbnail sketches the *Times* gave of each nominee, it was mentioned that the woman's husband was a professor of English. In the case of none of the other nominees was the existence of a spouse even hinted at, and much less was there any clue about the spouse's occupation. So here, although the existence of a husband was as irrelevant for this woman appointee as the existence of a wife was for any of the male appointees, the husband was mentioned, since a woman cannot be placed in her position in society by the readers of the *Times* unless they know her marital status. The same is not at all true of men. Similarly in the 1971 mayoral campaign in San Francisco, the sole woman candidate was repeatedly referred to as *Mrs. Feinstein,* never *Feinstein,* when her opponents were regularly referred to by first and last names or last names alone: *Joseph Alioto,* or *Alioto,* not *Mr. Alioto.* Again, the woman had to be identified by her relationship to a man, although this should bear no relevance to her qualifications for public office.

While sharp intellect is generally considered an unqualified virtue in a man, any character trait that is not related to a woman's utility to men is considered suspect, if not downright bad. Thus the word *brainy* is seldom used of men; when used of women it suggests (1) that this intelligence is unexpected in a woman; (2) that it isn't really a good trait. If one calls a woman "smart," outside of the sense of "fashionable," either one means it as a compliment to her domestic thrift and other housekeeping abilities or, again, it suggests a bit of wariness on the part of the speaker.

Also relevant here are the connotations (as opposed to the denotative meanings) of the words *spinster* and *bachelor.* Denotatively, these are, again, parallel to "cow" versus "bull": one is masculine, the other feminine, and both mean "one who is not married." But there the resemblance ends. *Bachelor* is at least a neutral term, often used as a compliment. *Spinster* normally seems to be used pejoratively, with connotations of prissiness, fussiness, and so on. Some of the differences between the two words are brought into focus in the following examples:

(22) *(a)* Mary hopes to meet an eligible bachelor.
     (b) *Fred hopes to meet an eligible spinster.

It is the concept of an *eligible spinster* that is anomalous. If someone is a spinster, by implication she is not eligible (to marry); she has had her chance, and been passed by. Hence, a girl of twenty cannot be properly called a spinster: she still has a chance to be married. (Of course, *spinster* may be used metaphorically in this situation, as described below.) But a man may be considered a bachelor as soon as he reaches marriageable age: to be a bachelor implies that one has the choice of marrying or not, and this is what makes the idea of a bachelor existence attractive, in the popular literature. He has been pursued and has successfully eluded his pursuers. But a spinster is one who has not been pursued, or at least not seriously. She is old unwanted goods. Hence it is not surprising to find that a euphemism has arisen for *spinster,* a word not much used today, *bachelor girl,* which attempts to capture for the woman the connotations *bachelor* has for a man. But this, too, is not much used except by writers trying to give their (slick magazine) prose a "with-it" sound. I have not heard the word used in unselfconscious speech. *Bachelor,* however, needs no euphemisms.

When *bachelor* and *spinster* are used metaphorically, the distinction in connotation between the two becomes even clearer:

(23) *(a)* John is a regular bachelor.
   (b) Mary is a regular spinster.

The metaphorical connotations of "bachelor" generally suggest sexual freedom; of "spinster," puritanism or celibacy. So we might use a sentence like (23)*(a)* if John was in fact married but engaged in extramarital affairs freely. It is hard to think of other circumstances in which it might be used. Certainly it could not be used if John were married but determined to remain celibate. (23) *(b),* on the other hand, might be used under two conditions: first, if Mary were in fact unmarried, but still of marriageable age (that is, not yet a literal spinster), and very cold and prissy; second, if Mary were married, with the same characteristics. The use of "regular," then, seems to be an indicator that the noun it modifies is to be taken purely in its connotative rather than denotative sense.

These examples could be multiplied. It is generally considered a *faux pas,* in proper society, to congratulate a girl on her engagement, while it is correct to congratulate her fiancé. Why is this? The reason here seems to be that it is impolite to remind someone of something that may be uncomfortable to him. To remind a girl that she must catch someone, that perhaps she might not have caught anyone, is rude, and this is what is involved, effectively, in congratulating someone. To congratulate someone is to rejoice with him in his good fortune; but it is not quite nice to remind a girl that getting married is good fortune for her, indeed a veritable necessity; it is too close to suggesting the bad fortune that it would be for her had she not found someone to marry. In the context of this society's assumptions about women's role, to congratulate a girl on her engagement is virtually to say, "Thank goodness! You had a close call!" For the man, on the other hand, there was no such danger. His choosing to marry is viewed as a good thing, but not something essential, and so he may be congratulated for doing a wise thing. If man and woman were equal in respect to marriage, it would be proper to congratulate either both or neither.

Another thing to think about is the traditional conclusion of the marriage service: "I now pronounce you man and wife." The man's position in the world, and in relation to other people including the bride, has not been changed by the act of marriage. He was a "man" before the ceremony, and a "man" he still is (one hopes) at its conclusion. But the bride went into the ceremony a "woman," not defined by any other person, at least linguistically; she leaves it a "wife," defined in terms of the "man," her husband. There are many other aspects of traditional marriage ceremonies in our culture that might be used to illustrate the same point.

And, having discussed bachelorhood and spinsterhood, and the marital state, we arrive at widowhood. Surely a bereaved husband and a bereaved wife are equivalent: they have both undergone the loss of a mate. But in fact, linguistically at any rate, this is not true. It is true that we have two words, *widow* and *widower;* but here again, *widow* is far commoner in use. Widows, not widowers, have their particular roles in folklore and tradition, and mourning behavior of particular sorts seems to be expected more strongly, and for a longer time, of a widow than of a widower. But there is more than this, as evidenced by the following:

(24) *(a)* Mary is John's widow.
    (b) *John is Mary's widower.

Like *mistress, widow* commonly occurs with a possessive preceding it, the name of the woman's late husband. Though he is dead, she is still defined by her relationship to him. But the bereaved husband is no longer defined in terms of his wife. While she is alive, he is sometimes defined as Mary's husband (though less often, probably, than she is as "John's wife"). But once she is gone, her function for him is over, linguistically speaking anyway. So once again, we see that women are always defined in terms of the men to whom they are related, and hence the worst thing that can happen to a woman is not to have a man in this relationship—that is, to be a spinster, a woman with neither husband nor lover, dead or alive.

What all these facts suggest is merely this, again: that men are assumed to be able to choose whether or not they will marry, and that therefore their not being married in no way precludes their enjoying sexual activity; but if a woman is not married, it is assumed to be because no one found her desirable. Hence if a woman is not married by the usual age, she is assumed to be sexually undesirable, prissy, and frigid.

The reason for this distinction seems to be found in the point made earlier: that women are given their identities in our society by virtue of their relationship with men, not vice versa.

It has been argued that this claim about disparities in use between *man/husband* and *woman/wife,* as well as *bachelor/spinster* and *widow/widower* does not apply in other languages, where they are not found, although otherwise the speakers of these languages are as sexist as any. Then, the argument continues, aren't these so-called proofs of linguistic sexism invalidated, in the face of, for example, the French *mari et femme* = "husband and woman"? Or in the face of the fact that *widower* is not morphologically marked vis-à-vis *widow,* in many languages?

My answer to all these arguments is *no.* We must look at the total picture, not its individual parts. Perhaps the French speaker says "*mari et femme*"; can a female speaker of French say "*mon mari travaille*"? Only if she can (and if a large body of the other claims made here are invalidated in French) can we claim that the linguistic disparity between "man" and "woman" does not hold in French.

Further, it should be clear that the *presence* of a marked trait (like the special ending on the masculine *widower*) is linguistic evidence of a social disparity; but the absence of such a trait is not evidence of its opposite. A language generally makes a distinction, or utilizes a marked form, for a reason; but the lack of such marking may be mere accident. Obviously, any fairly inventive mind, given fifteen minutes, could point to a dozen uses in English that are not sexist, but might conceivably have been so; but no one will use these nonoccurrences as proof of the nonsexism of English.

Now it becomes clearer why there is a lack of parallelism in men's and women's titles. To refer to a man as *Mr.* does not identify his marital status; but there is no such ambiguous term for women: one must decide on *Mrs.* or *Miss.* To remedy this imbalance, a bill was proposed in the United States Congress by Bella Abzug and others that would legislate a change in women's titles: *Miss* and *Mrs.* would both be abolished in favor of *Ms.* Rather less seriously, the converse has been proposed by Russell Baker, that two terms should be created for men, *Mrm.* and *Srs.,* depending upon marital status. We may ask several questions: *(a)* Why does the imbalance exist in the first place? *(b)* Why do we feel that Baker's suggestion (even if it did not come from Baker) is somehow not to be taken as seriously as Abzug's? And *(c)* does Abzug's proposal have a chance of being accepted in colloquial speech? (One must distinguish between acceptance in official use and documents, where Ms. is already used to some extent, and acceptance in colloquial conversation, where I have never heard it. I think the latter will be a long time in coming, and I do not think we can consider Ms. a real choice until this occurs.)

(a) A title is devised and used for a purpose: to give a clue to participants in social interaction how the other person is to be regarded, how he is to be addressed. In an avowedly class-conscious society, social ranking is a significant determining factor: once you know that your addressee is to be addressed as "lord," or "mister," or "churl," you know where he stands with respect to you; the title establishes his identity in terms of his relationship with the larger social group. For this reason, the recent suggestion that both *Mr.* and *Mrs./Miss* be abolished in favor of *Person* is unlikely to be successful: *Person* tells you only what you already know, and does not aid in establishing ranking or relationship between two people. Even in a supposedly classless society, the use of *Mr.* (as opposed to simple last

name or first name) connotes a great deal about the relationship of the two participants in the discourse with respect to each other. To introduce yourself, "I'm Mr. Jones" puts the relationship you are seeking to establish on quite a different basis than saying, "I'm Jones," or "I'm John," and each is usable under quite different contextual conditions, socially speaking. As long as social distinctions, overt or covert, continue to exist, we will be unable to rid our language of titles that make reference to them. It is interesting that the French and Russian revolutions both tried to do away with honorific titles that distinguished class by substituting "citizen(ess)" and "comrade." These, however, are not purely empty like "person": they imply that speaker and addressee share a relationship in that both are part of the state and hence, by implication, both equal. In France, the attempt was not long-lived. (Although *tovarishch* is normal today in the Soviet Union, I don't know whether it is really usable under all conditions, whether a factory worker, for instance, could use it to his foreman, or his foreman's wife.)

Although, in our society, naming conventions for men and women are essentially equal (both have first and last names, and both may have additional names, of lesser importance), the social conventions governing the choice of form of address is not parallel in both sexes. Thus, as noted, a man, Mr. John Jones, may be addressed as John, as Jones, as Mr. Jones, and as Mr. John Jones. The first normally implies familiarity, the second intimacy coupled with Jones's inferiority (except in situations of nondirect address, as in professional citation; or among intimates, as a possibly more intimate form of address even than first name alone, without inferiority being implied); the third distance and more or less equality. The last is never used in direct address, and again indicates considerable distance. To address someone by first name alone is to assume at least equality with the other person, and perhaps superiority (in which case the other person will respond with *Mr.* and last name). *Mr. Jones* is probably the least-marked form of address, a means of keeping distance with no necessary suggestions of status. To address someone as *Jones* socially or in business may be an indication of his inferior status, but to refer to someone that way professionally (as at a linguistics conference, generally in indirect reference rather than direct address) seems to be a mark of his acceptance, as a colleague and a person to be taken seriously as a fellow member of the profession. In this way, perhaps, it is related to the last-name-only of familiarity: it is "we know each other well; we are equals and pals, or equals and colleagues."

Possibly related to this is a discrepancy in the rules of professional naming. Among linguists, at any rate, there are rules, unwritten but generally understood, about when someone is referred to (orally in discussion, rather than cited in papers) by full name, by last name, by title (Dr., Professor, Mr.) plus last name. If one is speaking of a student, or of a close friend to someone else who, the speaker knows, is also a friend of the person referred to, and the name is unambiguous in context, the reference is often, though not necessarily, by first name, though one also hears last names if the person referred to is male: either *Fred* or *Smith* may be used to refer to Fred Smith under these circumstances. If the person is less well known, and therefore not considered somehow a full colleague, the reference is most often by full first and last name; *a paper by Smith's student, Bill Snurd,* not **Snurd.* (Any title alone with either last or first and last name indicates that the speaker himself is not a full member of the club or that he considers the person referred to beyond the professional pale: "Gosh, I talked to Professor Chomsky!" is the effusion of a neophyte.) All of this suggests a kind of understood camaraderie among people who are understood to "belong," and may act as a covert means of screening out nonmembers. Then what of the women in the profession (who, we will recall, are not professionals)? One finds oneself more and more often in awkward situations, as women become more prevalent in the field, and one does not know how to refer to them appropriately. If we are in a situation in which first name alone might be used of a male linguist, we are in no trouble: first name alone is used of a woman as well. If we are in a situation where first plus last name is used of a man, this will also be used for a woman, with no trouble. But there is a shadow area: if someone is assumed to be an equal and a colleague, but the speaker is not really a personal friend, or he knows the addressee is not, or he merely wishes to keep the conversation on a strictly impersonal note. Here, if the person referred to is a man, we normally find last name alone used. But for a woman, this is much less common. (I am, again, not referring to citation in writing, where last name alone is common for women as well as men.) There are two ways out: first name alone (Jane) or both names (Jane Jones), and I have encountered both, while I have virtually never encountered last name alone (Jones) for women. But the use of the first name alone, in situations in which it is not warranted, such as if the speaker really is not a personal friend with the person referred to, sounds patronizing, and the second awkward in suggesting that the person referred to is not accepted as a colleague. Yet these are the only normal options.

I am speaking here only of prevailing tendencies. Exceptions obviously exist, and are the more apt to be made the better known a woman is in her field. But certainly, in common conversational use among linguists speaking colloquially, we might expect to find sentence *(a)* below rather more than we might expect *(b)*.

Say, what did you think of Lakoff's latest paper, where *(a)* he
                                                          (b) she
makes the claim that logical structure is to be formally thought of as a 100-pound purple orangutan?

Ordinarily, the hearer of the sentence above would be somewhat jarred by encountering the feminine pronoun later in the sentence, since last name alone sets up a strong assumption that it is a male colleague being referred to. Probably the majority of linguists, in this situation, would also resort to circumlocution to avoid the following sentence:

(c) I understand Green is claiming that Morgan thinks with a fork.

It would seem as though male members of the profession are, subconsciously or otherwise, loath to admit women to full membership in their club, and this trouble in terms of address—limiting the choice to addressing a woman either by first name, in this situation implying her inferiority to the speaker, or by both names, suggesting she is not quite a full colleague—is symptomatic of deeper problems of which we are all aware.

I think this tendency to use first names sooner and be more apt to use them, rather than last name alone or title plus last name, in referring to and addressing women, is evident in other areas than academia. On television discussion shows, or commentary, or topical comedy (of the Bob Hope kind), a woman will be called or referred to by her first name where a man might not. Again, this is not a hard-and-fast rule, but depends upon the respect accorded to the woman due to her age, position, and attractiveness: it seems as though the more attractive a woman is, the less she can be taken seriously, and the more she is considered a decoration, able to be addressed by first name only. I feel that, other things being equal, there is a greater likelihood of hearing Gloria Steinem called "Gloria" by someone who does not know her very well than of hearing Norman Mailer called "Norman" under the same conditions. (Of course, nobody is likely to call the former Prime Minister of Israel "Golda.") This usage is perhaps to be compared with the tradition of calling children freely by their first names, and may be parallel to the use of "girl" for "woman" discussed earlier.

Aside from making apparent a dilemma arising from a social inequity, the facts noted above are of interest for other reasons: they show that titles are very much alive in our supposedly classless society, and apparently small differences in their use reflect great chasms in social position among users. The use (or misuse) of titles supplies much information to people, and hence titles are important in our language as in our society, and not about to be lightly discarded.

If then, we can reasonably assume that a title supplies information about the person to whose name it is attached, we may further assume that this information is necessary in telling people how to interact with this person. And if this sort of information is felt to be necessary for one class of people and not another, we may expect to find a distinction made in the titles for the first class, if at all, but not the second.

So it is with *Mrs., Miss,* and *Mr.* Since a significant part of the opinion one normally forms about a woman's character and social station depends on her marital status—as is not the case with men—it is obvious that the title of address should supply this information in the case of women, but not of men.

(It may seem as though a man's marital status is, under certain conditions, of crucial interest to a woman, and therefore this point is suspect. But I think we have to distinguish between importance in the eyes of a single person in a particular situation, and importance in the eyes of society at large, in a great many possible situations. At almost every turn, because of the way social and business events are arranged, one needs to know a woman's marital status, and the position held by her husband. But one does not need the same information about a man, since his social status can be gauged, generally, purely by reference to his own accomplishments.) Once again, it would seem that trying to legislate a change in a lexical item is fruitless. The change to *Ms.* will not be generally adopted until a woman's status in society changes to assure her an identity based on her own accomplishments. (Perhaps even more debasing than the *Mrs./Miss* distinction is the fact that the woman in marrying relinquishes her own name, while the man does not. This suggests even more firmly that a woman is her husband's possession, having no other identity than that of his wife. Not only does she give up her last name [which, after all, she took from her father], but often her first name as well, to become *Mrs. John Smith.*)

Although blacks are not yet fully accorded equal status with whites in this society, nevertheless *black,* a term coined to elicit racial pride and sense of unity, seems to have been widely adopted both by blacks and whites, both in formal use and in the media, and increasingly in colloquial conversation. Does this constitute a counterexample to my claim here? I think not, but rather an element of hope. My point is that linguistic and social change go hand in hand: one cannot, purely by changing language use, change social status. The word *black,* in its current sense, was not heard until the late 1960s or even 1970, to any significant extent. I think if its use had been proposed much earlier, it would have failed in acceptance. I think the reason people other than blacks can understand and sympathize with black racial pride is that they were made aware of the depths of their prejudice during the civil rights struggles of the early 1960s. It took nearly ten years from the beginning of this struggle for the use of *black* to achieve wide acceptance, and it is still often used a bit self-consciously, as though italicized. But since great headway was made first in the social sphere, linguistic progress could be made *on that basis;* and now this linguistic progress, it is hoped, will lead to new social progress in turn. The women's movement is but a few years old, and has, I should think, much deeper ingrained hostility to overcome than the civil rights movement ever did. (Among the intelligentsia, the black civil rights struggle was never a subject for ridicule, as women's liberation all too often is, among those very liberals who were the first on their blocks to join the NAACP.) The parallel to the black struggle should indicate that social change must precede lexical change: women must achieve some measure of greater social independence of men before *Ms.* can gain wider acceptance.

(b) There is thus a very good reason why a distinction is made in the case of women, but not men, in the matter of marital status. But this fact suggests an answer to the second question posed above, regarding why *Ms.* is felt to be a more serious proposal than Baker's suggestion. It is obviously easier to imagine obliterating an extant distinction than creating a new one: easier to learn to ignore the marital status of a woman than to begin to pay attention to that of a man. Moreover, we may also assume that for a woman, the use of *Ms.* is a liberating device, one to be desired. But (as Baker suggests) the use of two titles for men is an encumbrance, a remover of certain kinds of liberties, and something definitely undesirable. So the two suggestions are not equivalent, and if either were ever to be accepted, the choice of *Ms.* is the probable candidate.

(c) The third question regarding the chances *Ms.* has for real acceptance has, in effect, already been answered. Until society changes so that the distinction between married and unmarried women is as unimportant in terms of their social position as that between married and unmarried men, the attempt in all probability cannot succeed. Like the attempt to substitute any euphemism for an uncomfortable word, the attempt to do away with *Miss* and *Mrs.* is doomed to failure if it is not accompanied by a change in society's attitude to what the titles describe.

4 / Conclusion

Linguistic imbalances are worthy of study because they bring into sharper focus real-world imbalances and inequities. They are clues that some external situation needs changing, rather than items that one *should* seek to change directly. A competent doctor tries to eliminate the germs that cause measles, rather than trying to bleach the red out with peroxide. I emphasize this point because it seems to be currently fashionable to try, first, to attack the disease by attempting to obliterate the external symptoms; and, second, to attack *every* instance of linguistic sexual inequity, rather than selecting those that reflect a real disparity in social treatment, not mere grammatical nonparallelism. We should be attempting to single out those linguistic uses that, by implication and innuendo, demean the members of one group or another, and should be seeking to make speakers of English aware of the psychological damage such forms do. The problem, of course, lies in deciding which forms are really damaging to the ego, and then in determining what to put in their stead.

A good example, which troubles me a lot at present, is that of pronominal neutralization. In English, as indeed in the great majority of the world's languages, when reference is made individually to members of a sexually mixed group, the normal solution is to resolve the indecision as to pronoun choice in favor of the masculine:[4] the

4. Wallace Chafe has given me an interesting example relative to this discussion of pronominal neutralization and sexism. In Iroquoian, neutralization is through the use of the feminine pronoun. The Iroquoian society is sometimes (inaccurately) referred to as matriarchal; in any case, women play a special role. These two facts together would seem to be a vindication for those who claim that neutralization in favor of the masculine pronoun, as in English, is a mark of the sexism rampant in our culture. But elsewhere in Iroquoian, this claim is belied. There are numerous prefixes attached to nouns, distinguishing number, gender, and case. When the noun refers to masculine human beings, these prefixes are kept separate of one another. But in referring to feminine human beings, animals, and inanimate objects, these numerous prefixes may be collapsed. This suggests that here women are considered in the category of animals and things, and lower or less important than men, contradicting the implications of the pronominal system. So this shows that even in a matriarchal society, sexism exists and

masculine, then, is "unmarked" or "neutral," and therefore will be found referring to men and women both in sentences like the following:

(25) *(a)* Everyone take his seat.

     (b) If a person wants to ingratiate himself with Harry, he

                                 *herself   *she

     should cook him moo-shu pork.

In (25) *(a)*, *her* could of course be used in an all-female group; the point is that in a mixed group, even one predominantly female, *his* will normally be the "correct" form. Many speakers, feeling this is awkward and perhaps even discriminatory, attempt a neutralization with *their,* a usage frowned upon by most authorities as inconsistent or illogical. In (25) *(b), herself* and *she* might conceivably replace *himself* and *he,* but the effect of the sentence would be changed, not too surprisingly: the ingratiation would be understood as an attempt at (sexual) seduction, or an attempt to persuade Henry to marry the "person."

That is, although semantically both men and women are included in the groups referred to by the pronouns in these sentences, only *he* and related masculine forms are commonly possible. An analogous situation occurs in many languages with the words for *human being:* in English, we find *man* and *mankind,* which of course refer to women members of the species as well. This of course permits us innumerable jokes involving "man-eating sharks," and the widespread existence of these jokes perhaps points up the problem that these forms create for a woman who speaks a language like English.

I feel that the emphasis upon this point, to the exclusion of most other linguistic points, by writers within the women's movement is misguided. While this lexical and grammatical neutralization is related to the fact that men have been the writers and the doers, I don't think it by itself specifies a particular and demeaning role for

has grammatical reflexes. It also suggests that pronoun neutralization is not really the crucial issue: there are other aspects of language—in English as well as Iroquoian— which are better indicators of the relationship between linguistic usage and cultural assumptions.

women, as the special uses of *mistress* or *professional,* to give a few examples, do. It is not insidious in the same way: it does not indicate to little girls how they are expected to behave. Even if it did, surely other aspects of linguistic imbalance should receive equal attention. But more seriously, I think one should force oneself to be realistic: certain aspects of language are available to the native speakers' conscious analysis, and others are too common, too thoroughly mixed throughout the language, for the speaker to be aware each time he uses them. It is realistic to hope to change only those linguistic uses of which speakers themselves can be made aware, as they use them. One chooses, in speaking or writing, more or less consciously and purposefully among nouns, adjectives, and verbs; one does not choose among pronouns in the same way. My feeling is that this area of pronominal neutralization is both less in need of changing and less open to change than many of the other disparities that have been discussed earlier, and we should perhaps concentrate our efforts where they will be most fruitful.

But many nonlinguists disagree. I have read and heard dissenting views from too many anguished women to suppose that this use of *he* is really a triviality. The claim is that the use of the neutral *he* with such frequency makes women feel shut out, not a part of what is being described, an inferior species, or a nonexistent one. Perhaps linguistic training has dulled my perception, and this really is a troublesome question. If so, I don't know what to advise, since I feel in any case that an attempt to change pronominal usage will be futile. My recommendation then would be based purely on pragmatic considerations: attempt to change only what can be changed, since this is hard enough.

I think in any case that linguists should be consulted before any more fanciful plans are made public for reforming the inequities of English. Many of these are founded on misunderstanding and create well-deserved ridicule, but this ridicule is then carried over into other areas which are not ludicrous at all, but suffer guilt by association. For instance, there have been serious suggestions lately that women have not had much influence on the affairs of the world because the term for the thing is *his-tory.* They suggest that the problem could be solved by changing the word to *her-story.*

It should not be necessary to spend time demolishing this proposal, but it is so prevalent that it must be stopped soon. First of all, the argument at very best confuses cause and effect: it is very seldom the case that a certain form of behavior results from being given a certain name, but rather, names are given on the basis of previously observed behavior. So anteaters are so called because they were observed to eat ants; it is not the case that the name "anteater" was given them randomly, and they rewarded the giver of the name by eating ants, which they had not previously done. But in any event, the argument is fallacious. The word *history* is not derived from two English words, *his + story;* rather it comes from the Greek word *historia,* from a root meaning "know." The Greeks, in coining the word, did not think it had anything to do with men versus women; so it could not have been so called because men were the only ones who played a part in it, nor could it have been so called in order to ensure that only men would have this role. In many languages, the equivalent of the English word *history* is related to it in appearance and origin; yet in none of them does it appear related in any way to the masculine pronoun (cf. French *histoire*). Yet the world's history is the same for speakers of all languages, generally speaking. This kind of thinking is both ludicrous and totally fallacious, and is discussed at undeserved length here only because the attention it has received has distracted people from thinking of more serious problems. And more recently still, I have read a suggestion that hurricanes be renamed *himicanes,* since the former appellation reflects poorly on women. If this sort of stuff appears in print and in the popular media as often as it does, it becomes increasingly more difficult to persuade men that women are really rational beings.

If we can accept the facts already discussed as generally true, for most people, most of the time, then we can draw from them several conclusions, of interest to readers in any of various fields.

1. People working in the women's liberation movement, and other social reformers, can see that there *is* a discrepancy between English as used by men and by women; and that the social discrepancy in the positions of men and women in our society is reflected in linguistic

disparities. The linguist, through linguistic analysis, can help to pin-point where these disparities lie, and can suggest ways of telling when improvements have been made. But it should be recognized that social change creates language change, not the reverse; or at best, language change influences changes in attitudes slowly and indirectly, and these changes in attitudes will not be reflected in social change unless society is receptive already. Further, the linguist can suggest which linguistic disparities reflect real and serious social inequalities; which are changeable, which will resist change; and can thus help the workers in the real world to channel their energies most constructively and avoid ridicule.

2. For the teacher of second languages, it is important to realize that social context is relevant in learning to speak a second language fluently. It is also important for a teacher to be aware of the kind of language he or she is speaking: if a woman teacher unconsciously teaches "women's language" to her male students, they may be in difficulties when they try to function in another country; if a female anthropologist learns the "men's language" of an area, she may not be able to get anywhere with the inhabitants because she seems un-feminine, and they will not know how to react to her. Language learning thus goes beyond phonology, syntax, and semantics, but it takes a perceptive teacher to notice the pitfalls and identify them correctly for students.

3. And finally, we have something for the theoretical linguist to consider. We have been talking about the use of language: what can be more germane than this in formulating a theory of language? We have shown that language use changes depending on the position in society of the language user, that a sentence that is "acceptable" when uttered by a woman is "unacceptable" when uttered by a man, or that one sentence may be "acceptable" under one set of assumptions in the subject matter, "unacceptable" under another. That is, it is a mistake to hope (as earlier linguistic theories have sometimes done) that the acceptability of a sentence is a yes-no or */non* decision: rather we must think in terms of hierarchies of grammaticality, in which the acceptability of a sentence is determined through the combination of many factors: not only the phonology, the syntax, and the semantics,

but also the social context in which the utterance is expressed, and the assumptions about the world made by all the participants in the discourse. It is sometimes objected that this is the realm of "pragmatics," not "linguistics," that it reflects "performance," not "competence." My feeling is that language use by any other name is still linguistics, and it is the business of the linguist to tell why and where a sentence is acceptable, and to leave the name-calling to the lexicographers. If a linguist encounters an example like *The way prices are rising is horrendous, isn't it?* and feels indecisive about its acceptability in various situations, it is his duty to tell exactly where his doubts lie, and why. It is as important for him to catalog the contextual situations under which a tag question like this (or tag questions in general) may be used as to determine the syntactic environment in which the tag question formation rule may apply. To stop with the latter (as is done, for example, in standard transformational grammar) is to tell half the story.

Or to take another instance: we have discussed a wide variety of problematical cases. Why can't you say: *John is Mary's widower?* (And this sentence is bad under *any* conditions, and hence is not a question of "performance.") Why have the meanings of *master* and *mistress* changed in a nonparallel fashion over time? Why does *He's a professional* have different implications than *She's a professional?* Suppose a linguist wishes to avoid making reference to social context in his grammar. How can he deal with such cases? First, there is the problem of the nonparallelism in the use of *widow* and *widower*. He might mark the latter in his lexicon as [—NPgenitive——] or a similar ad hoc device. Or one might say that *widow* had underlying it a 2-place predicate, while there was a 1-place predicate underlying *widower*. That this is ludicrous, in that it distorts the meaning of the latter sentence, is evident. In the case of *professional*, the theorist who excludes social context would have a slightly different problem. He has to indicate in the lexicon that there are two words *professional*, presumably accidental homonyms. One is restricted to women, like *pregnant;* the other is restricted to men, like *virile*. (Of course, there are obvious semantic reasons, going back to facts in the real world, in the cases of *pregnant* and *virile* that make their gender restrictions non-ad hoc. Since this is not the case with *professional,* he has already introduced arbitrariness into this lexical item.) Then one sense of *professional,* the one restricted to women, is defined as: "lit. or fig., a prostitute." The other sense, specific to men, is defined: "engaging in certain business activities . . ." or whatever. And similarly, he would in the case of *master* and *mistress* have to construct a very strange theory of historical change in order to allow these words to diverge in sense in the way in which they have.

This is not to say that these facts cannot be handled in some ad hoc fashion; my point here is merely that to take such a course is to violate the principles of valid linguistic description. First, the linguist taking this position has been forced to resort to numerous ad hoc devices purely in order to avoid generating impossible sentences while generating those that are grammatical. Second, and perhaps more seriously, he would be overlooking the real point of what is going on. Each of the nonparallelisms that have been discussed here (as well, of course, as the many others I have mentioned elsewhere, and still others the reader can no doubt supply himself) would in such treatment be nonparallel for a different reason from each of the others. Yet the speaker of English who has not been raised in a vacuum *knows* that all of these disparities exist in English for the same reason: *each reflects in its pattern of usage the difference between the role of women in our society and that of men.* If there were tomorrow, say by an act of God, a total restructuring of society as we know it so that women were in fact equal to men, we would make certain predictions about the future behavior of the language. One prediction we might make is that *all* these words, together, would cease to be nonparallel. If the curious behavior of each of these forms were idiosyncratic, we would not expect them to behave this way en masse. If their peculiarity had nothing to do with the way society was organized, we would not expect their behavior to change as a result of social change. Now of course, one cannot prove points by invoking a cataclysmic change that has not occurred and, in all probability, will not. But I do think an appeal is possible to the reader's intuition: this seems a likely way for these forms to behave. In any event, I think this much is clear: that there is a generalization that can be made regarding the aberrant behavior of all these lexical items, but this generalization can be made only by reference, in the grammar of the language, to social mores. The linguist must involve himself, professionally, with sociology: first, because he is able to isolate the data that the sociologist can use in determining the weaknesses and strengths of a culture (as we have done, to some extent, here); and then because if he does not examine the society of the speakers of the language along with the so-called purely linguistic data, he will be unable to make the relevant generalizations, will be unable to understand why the language works the way it does. He will, in short, be unable to do linguistics.[5]

5. This is not the only known situation in which the linguist must work with the concepts of sociology. To give another example, in his paper "Anaphoric Islands" in Binnick et al., eds., *Papers from the Fifth Regional Meeting of the Chicago Linguistic Society,* May 1969, Postal discusses the distribution of terms like *dogmeat, wombatmeat, pigmeat* (as opposed to *dog, chicken, pork*). He suggests that *-meat* must appear if the item is not regularly eaten by the speakers of the language. This is another example in which reference must be made to purely cultural, extralinguistic facts about a society in order to judge the well-formedness of lexical items.

PART II

Why Women Are Ladies

1 / Introduction

In the preceding discussion, I talked at some length about the linguistic uses that characterize traditional "women's language," as well as the ways in which we speak differently of women than of men. I tried to give evidence that the discrepancies that appear to exist are harmful to women's self-image and to the image people in general form of women's character and abilities.

One of the problems I have run into in presenting these ideas is that often, while everyone acknowledges the existence of nonparallel usages such as the ones I described, people also feel that no inequity exists; men and women are "separate but equal," and no redress need be made; *vive,* in fact, *la différence.* In addition, people very often feel affronted at my criticisms—this is true of both men and women—because they have been taught that the discrepancies actually favor women, and here I am trying to change them; I am striking a blow against womankind and maybe even mankind, since it benefits women and everyone else to have these distinctions. The argument most often revolves around the notions of "politeness" we were all taught as children: women's speech differs from men's in that women are more polite, which is precisely as it should be, since women are the preservers of morality and civility; and we speak around women in an especially "polite" way in return, eschewing the coarseness of ruffianly men's language: no slang, no swear words, no off-color remarks. Further, many of the ways we choose to speak of women reflect our higher estimate of them than of men, and exalt and flatter, rather than humiliate. So, the argument runs, my position, that women should be aware of these discrepancies in language and do what they can to demolish them, is the one that denigrates and degrades women.

I appreciate the superficial force of that argument; and certainly, if a woman feels she has no other strength or status in the real world than as "lady," arbiter of morality, judge of manners, she might well be affronted by the comments I make. My hope is that women will recognize that such a role is insufficient for a human being and will then realize that using this language, having it used of them, and thus being placed implicitly in this role, is degrading in that it is constraining. There's nothing wrong, obviously, with having a natural sense of rhythm; but to impute this quality, sight unseen, to *all* blacks and thus to each black in turn that one encounters is insulting. Similarly, if some women want to be arbiters of morality, that's fine with me; but I don't like the idea that, because I came into the world with two X chromosomes, I have no choice but to be an arbiter of morality, and will automatically be treated as though I were.

Hence this discussion. What I want to talk about is precisely the relationship between women's language, language referring to women, and politeness and to reflect on the reasons behind this relationship. The question is complicated by the fact that politeness is many-faceted, just as there are many forms of women's language and many distinctions among the uses so identified in the preceding part of this book. For instance, almost no one I know of my age and general educational status would be caught dead saying "divine," and some even claim not to be able to identify "magenta," while knowing what a universal joint is (in their car, rather than their roach clip). But question intonation in declarative-requiring situations is very common among us still, and much as we feel the need to extirpate it, it flourishes as long as we don't have perfect self-confidence. Using "divine" is not a mark of feelings of inferiority, but rather a mere badge of class—female class. Using question intonation inappropriately is both. The latter dies harder than the former.

Similarly, as I shall discuss at length, there are many types of behavior that can be called "polite." Some forms of politeness are linguistic, some purely nonlinguistic, and many mixed; some are polite in some settings, neutral or downright rude in others; some are polite in some societies, rude in others; and finally some are polite in some societies at one stage of a relationship, but rude in another society at a parallel stage, perhaps polite in the latter society at a different stage. What I will propose are some tentative "working rules" for the types of politeness that are found and an attempt to describe the situations in which each is appropriate. I will then talk about the relationship between women's language and language about women, and these rules of politeness, as compared to and contrasted with what one finds in men's and in neutral language. Finally I will offer some rather tentative speculations on what is possibly going on: why the discrepancies exist, and why they are deleterious to society in general as well as to women in particular, and are not the innocent flattery they are thought of as being.

Let me summarize here for convenience the forms that I see as comprising "women's language," most of which have already been discussed at length.

1. Women have a large stock of words related to their specific interests, generally relegated to them as "woman's work": magenta, shirr, dart (in sewing), and so on. If men use these words at all, it tends to be tongue-in-cheek.

2. "Empty" adjectives like *divine, charming, cute. . . .*

3. Question intonation where we might expect declaratives: for instance tag questions ("It's so hot, isn't it?") and rising intonation in statement contexts ("What's your name, dear?" "Mary Smith?").

4. The use of hedges of various kinds. Women's speech seems in general to contain more instances of "well," "y'know," "kinda," and so forth: words that convey the sense that the speaker is uncertain about what he (or she) is saying, or cannot vouch for the accuracy of the statement. These words are fully legitimate when, in fact, this is the case (for example, if one says, "John is sorta tall," meaning he's neither really impressively tall nor actually short, but rather middling,

though toward the tall side: 5 feet 9 rather than 6 feet 5, say). There is another justifiable use in which the hedge mitigates the possible unfriendliness or unkindness of a statement—that is, where it's used for the sake of politeness. Thus, "John is sorta short," where I mean: He's 5 feet 2 and you're 5 feet 8, Mary, so how will it look if you go out with him? Here, I know exactly how short he is, and it is very short, but I blunt the force of a rather painful assertion by using the hedge. What I mean is the class of cases in which neither of these facts pertains, and a hedge shows up anyway: the speaker is perfectly certain of the truth of the assertion, and there's no danger of offense, but the tag appears anyway as an apology for making an assertion at all. Anyone may do this if he lacks self-confidence, as everyone does in some situations; but my impression is that women do it more, precisely because they are socialized to believe that asserting themselves strongly isn't nice or ladylike, or even feminine. Another manifestation of the same thing is the use of "I guess" and "I think" prefacing declarations or "I wonder" prefacing questions, which themselves are hedges on the speech-acts of saying and asking. "I guess" means something like: I would like to say . . . to you, but I'm not sure I can (because I don't know if it's right, because I don't know if I have the right, because I don't know how you'd take it, and so on), so I'll merely put it forth as a suggestion. Thus, if I say, "It will rain this afternoon," and it doesn't, you can later take me to task for a misleading or inaccurate prediction. But if I say, "I guess it will rain this afternoon," then I am far less vulnerable to such an attack. So these hedges do have their uses when one really has legitimate need for protection, or for deference (if we are afraid that by making a certain statement we are overstepping our rights), but used to excess, hedges, like question intonation, give the impression that the speaker lacks authority or doesn't know what he's talking about. Again, these are familiar misogynistic criticisms, but the use of these hedges arises out of a fear of seeming too masculine by being assertive and saying things directly.

5. Related to this is the use of the intensive "so." Again, this is more frequent in women's than men's language, though certainly men can use it. Here we have an attempt to hedge on one's strong feelings, as

though to say: I feel strongly about this—but I dare not make it clear *how* strong. To say, "I like him very much," would be to say precisely that you like him to a great extent. To say, "I like him *so* much" weasels on that intensity: again, a device you'd use if you felt it unseemly to show you had strong emotions, or to make strong assertions, but felt you had to say something along those lines anyway.

6. Hypercorrect grammar: women are not supposed to talk rough. It has been found that, from a very young age, little boys "drop" their *g*'s much more than do little girls: boys say "singin'," "goin'," and so on, while girls are less apt to. Similarly little boys are less apt than little girls to be scolded for saying "ain't" or at least they are scolded less severely, because "ain't" is more apt to remain in their vocabularies than in their sisters'. Generally women are viewed as being the preservers of literacy and culture, at least in Middle America, where literacy and culture are viewed as being somewhat suspect in a male. (That is, in cultures where learning is valued for itself, men are apt to be the guardians of culture and the preservers of grammar; in cultures where book larnin' is the schoolmarm's domain, this job will be relegated to the women. Jespersen remarks somewhere that women are more prone to neologism than men and hence more likely to be the originators of linguistic change; but I think he was thinking in terms of European society of the last century, where indeed the men were virtually always more highly educated than the women, and education a mark of status.)

7. Superpolite forms. This is the point alluded to earlier: women are supposed to speak more politely than men. This is related to their hypercorrectness in grammar, of course, since it's considered more mannerly in middle-class society to speak "properly." But it goes deeper: women don't use off-color or indelicate expressions; women are the experts at euphemism; more positively, women are the repositories of tact and know the right things to say to other people, while men carelessly blurt out whatever they are thinking. Women are supposed to be particularly careful to say "please" and "thank you" and to uphold the other social conventions; certainly a woman who fails at these tasks is apt to be in more trouble than a man who does so: in a man it's "just like a man," and indulgently overlooked unless

his behavior is really boorish. In a woman, it's social death in conventional circles to refuse to go by the rules.

8. Women don't tell jokes. As we shall see in a while, this point is just an elaboration of the two immediately preceding. But it is axiomatic in middle-class American society that, first, women can't tell jokes—they are bound to ruin the punchline, they mix up the order of things, and so on. Moreover, they don't "get" jokes. In short, women have no sense of humor.

9. Women speak in italics, and the more ladylike and feminine you are, the more in italics you are supposed to speak. This is another way of expressing uncertainty with your own self-expression, though this statement may appear contradictory: italics, if anything, seem to *strengthen* (note those italics) an utterance. But actually they say something like: Here are directions telling you how to react, since my saying something by itself is not likely to convince you: I'd better use double force, to make sure you see what I mean. It is well known, for instance, that beginning students in English composition tend to use italics far more than do established and confident writers of prose, precisely because the former are afraid, even as they write, that they are not being listened to, that their words are apt to have no effect.

There are doubtless other devices that are parts of women's language. Some can't be described in writing because there is no easy way to give examples: this is true of specifically female intonation patterns. Certainly it can be said that women have at their disposal a wider range of intonation patterns than do men, both within sentences and among full-sentence patterns. I am not sure why this is so. Possibly extra intonational variety is used as a sort of secondary signal, in case the first was not received. That is, if you have reason to be afraid you're not being listened to, or not being taken seriously, you will throw in extra ways for the hearer to figure out what you've said— you'll try every means to ensure that your message is received and responded to. (Thus, if you're speaking to someone you are afraid doesn't understand English very well, you'll be more prone to resort to gestures than you would be if there was no language problem.) Perhaps women realize that they are often not being listened to, because obviously they couldn't be saying anything that really mattered, and therefore, more or less consciously, use voice patterns that have a dual effect: first, of being very attention-catching in the hope that if what you have to say won't be perceived, at least the addressee will hear how you're saying it; and then, since pitch and stress carry some semantic force, the speaker may hope that some of the message will percolate through by that means, though it might be lost if stated only once, by words alone. It may be for this reason as well that women are more prone to gesture as they speak than are men. All this is speculation, though I think interesting speculation.

A first objection that might occur to these points is that men *can* use virtually every item on this list; some men, surely, use none, some use some, and some maybe even use all. The latter is very often the case with academic men; and I think that the decisive factor is less purely gender than power in the real world. But it happens that, as a result of natural gender, a woman tends to have, and certainly tends to feel she has, little real-world power compared with a man; so generally a woman will be more apt to have these uses than a man will. It is equally true that different women speak women's language to differing extents; and interestingly enough, it seems that academic women are among the least apt to be speakers of this language. But this may be because women who have succeeded in academe have more power than other women who have no outside roles; and that in determining their real-world power, women use as a basis the power of the men they know. Since the men that women academics are most likely to know are male academics, on this basis of comparison, with the relatively real-world-powerless, they seem to have more power than other women, so they are less apt to have to resort to women's language. And, in my experience, academia is a more egalitarian society than most, in terms of sex roles and expectations.

In any event, it should be clear that I am not talking about hundred-percent correlations, but rather, general tendencies. If you are a woman, it is more likely that you will speak this way than if you are a man, but that is not to say that I predict you do speak this way if you're a woman, or don't if you're a man. Further, you could speak this way to some extent; or could speak it under some circumstances but not others. (For instance, in the office where you're in charge you might avoid it, but might use it habitually at home, perhaps not even realizing you are making the switch.)

It has recently been suggested by Cheris Kramer (in *Psychology Today,* June 1974) that these claims are inaccurate. Her reason is this: that in questionnaires that they filled out, women did not indicate that they used "women's" language nor did men indicate that they necessarily considered these traits peculiar to women. There are several things to be said in reply to this. First, it has never been claimed— as I have said already—that men can't use these forms, or that women must. What I have said is that women use them, or are likely to use them, in a wider range of linguistic, psychological, and social environments—that women typically lack assertiveness, for one thing, in more contexts than men do. (Obviously there will be exceptions.) Second, the device of the interview in these cases is suspect. Asking people how they feel about linguistic forms makes them self-conscious about them; they may feel that if they say "yes," they will be disapproved of, or that you're not a nice person if you don't answer "right," however "right" may be construed in a given instance. This may not even be explicitly realized but can skew the figures all the same. And very often, people simply aren't aware of what they say; it takes a trained linguist to have the "ear" for that. And it is probably true that the more potentially embarrassing the questions are, the more distortion (whether conscious or not) can be expected. And questions raising concern over one's masculinity or femininity, or the proper role for one's sex, are certainly embarrassing. So it's unsafe to take such a questionnaire at face value.

Another problem with many tests that have been made for recognition of "women's language" is that they have depended on written samples (one example I know of used freshman composition themes). Not too surprisingly, these tests tend to show that little or no correlation is found by the subjects between the sex of the actual writer of the piece and the sex ascribed to him or her. This finding, however, is deceptive.

If you look at the list of distinguishing criteria for women's language that I gave earlier, you will note that most of the characteristics are apt to be found only in spoken, or at least highly informal, style.

This is because they are *personal* markers: they signal to the addressee how the speaker feels about what she (he, of course, in the analogous cases of men's language) is saying, and how the speaker hopes or expects that the hearer will react. Such commentary is a part of *informal* style—person-to-person friendly speech, and sometimes, though increasingly rarely these days, letters—rather than formal style—lectures and most forms of writing. In particular, freshman composition style is notorious for its awkward formality, owing to uneasiness in writing, and is the last place one would look for personal characterization, indicative of the writer's feeling of comfortable rapport with a potential reader.

Cartoon captions, minus the cartoons of course, which have also been used as a testing device, will also produce suspect results, because they are not part of connected dialogue and because they are contextless. The criteria I listed above were *not* intended as yes-or-no certainties. What I said was that most women would use most of them in a wider range of psychological and social environments than most men would (a very hedgy statement, but what did you expect?), because women tend to feel unwilling to assert themselves in a wider range of circumstances than men do. Hence, one can judge whether something is "women's language," "men's language," or "neutral" only with reference to the real-world context in which it was uttered—a complex and subtle combination of judgments that would be virtually impossible to reproduce in a natural way in an experimental situation.

There's another point, and that is that a stereotypical image may be far more influential than a (mere) statistical correlation. Let's say, for the sake of argument, that *no* real female person in the United States actually speaks any form or dialect of women's language. Yet there are the innumerable women we see on television, who whether we like it or not form role models for young girls. Maybe Edith Bunker is not presented as a wholly believable or admirable figure, but certainly she is presented as a conceivable female type, one that someone might eventually aspire to fit into. Edith Bunker is obviously an extreme case, but almost every woman you see in the media has many traits of women's language built into her speech. And these stereotypical women, I fear, have great influence over the young: I recall, as a child, worrying because I didn't fit the pattern for which women were being ridiculed in jokes I heard on television. I wasn't fuzzy-minded, I didn't care if another girl at a party wore the same dress I did, I wasn't extravagant, and so on. It frightened rather than cheered me to realize this discrepancy between the female stereotype and myself: I feared I'd never make it. True, I didn't (at least I hope I didn't) remake myself to fit the stereotype, but seeing that image there continually in a thousand variations did nothing for my self-image: first, because that was the *best* I, as a girl, could hope to aspire to; second, and maybe worse, because I couldn't even manage *that* role. Maybe I was especially vulnerable, but I feel that the stereotypes we see in the media are far more influential than we like to think they are, and they should be taken very seriously indeed.

Another thing I have sometimes been accused of saying, and would take exception to, is that women have all the problems, that it's easy for men: *they* aren't constrained or bound into roles; their lives are simple. Nothing is further from the truth, or my mind. Larry Josephson has shown, in an unpublished paper discussing men's language, that men are just as constrained in what they are supposed, and not supposed, to say as are women. For instance, men in most occupations and social strata may *not* use empty adjectives or let on that they know the meanings of words like "kick pleat" or "braise." If men are too grammatical or too polite in their speech, they are viewed with suspicion. Men are supposed to be in command of a whole different range of lexical items, and woe betide a man in some circles if he doesn't know the name and function of everything in his car. He generally is expected to know how to swear and how to tell and appreciate the telling of dirty jokes, and certainly must never giggle when he hears them.

Constraining as all this is, I feel it is constraining in a less damaging way than are the confines of women's language on its speakers. The question to ask is: What happens to people who are taught to speak the language, and then speak it? What are the rewards?

If a man learns to speak men's language, and is otherwise unambiguously placed in his society as a man, his is a relatively (and I say only *relatively*) simple position. His rewards, in the traditional culture, are easy to see. He is listened to and taken seriously; he becomes one of the boys and can engage in various kinds of camaraderie, achieving closeness to his buddies by the language all share, the slang and dirty jokes bringing them closer to each other. His learning of his proper language brings purely positive results, in terms of how people react to the way he talks.

Not so for the woman. If she doesn't learn to speak women's language, in traditional society she's dead: she is ostracized as unfeminine by both men and women. So that is not a possible option, unless a young girl is exceedingly brave—in fact, reckless. But what if she opts to do as she ought—learn to talk like a lady? She has some rewards: she is accepted as a suitable female. But she also finds that she is treated—purely because of the way she speaks and, therefore, supposedly thinks—as someone not to be taken seriously, of dim intelligence, frivolous, and incapable of understanding anything important. It is true that some women seem to adapt to this role quite nicely, and indeed it has apparent advantages: if you're not taken seriously, if you can't understand anything, you then have no responsibility for important ideas, you don't have to trouble your pretty little head about deep problems. Maybe this is nice for a while, but surely it's hard to be a child forever. If a woman learns and uses women's language, she is necessarily considered less than a real, full person— she's a bit of fluff.

Now that means, as I said already, that a woman is damned if she does and damned if she doesn't. And this is a form of the paradox that Gregory Bateson has called a double-bind: a double-bind is a situation in which a person, by obeying an order, automatically disobeys it. Further, the order is given in a situation in which it cannot be questioned—it is given by too potent an authority. The classical example is that of the soldier who is ordered to cut the hair of everyone in the regiment except those who cut their own. The dilemma arises when he comes to consider his own hair. Whichever path he chooses—to cut his hair or not to—he disobeys one part of the order. Now the command that society gives to the young of both sexes might be phrased something like: "Gain respect by speaking like other members of your sex." For the boy, as we have seen, that order, constraining as it is, is not paradoxical: if he speaks (and generally behaves) as men in his culture are supposed to, he generally gains people's respect. But whichever course the woman takes—to speak women's language or not to—she will not be respected. So she cannot carry out the order, and the order is transmitted by society at large; there is no way to question it, no one even to direct the question to. Bateson claims that if someone is exposed to a double-bind in childhood, he may become schizophrenic and that, indeed, double-binds are found in many schizophrenogenic families.

Now clearly it would be ridiculous to claim that therefore women are typically schizophrenic in a clinical sense. But certainly it is true that more women than men are institutionalized for mental illness; women form the huge majority of psychiatric patients. It may be that men and women start out with the same psychological equipment, but fighting the paradoxes a woman necessarily faces tends to break down a woman's mental resources; therefore a woman is more apt to run into mental difficulties and, when she faces real stress, to have fewer inner resources left to overcome her problems. So it is just possible that society is putting a far greater strain on its women than on its men, and it is time to ask whether this is true, and if true, how the burden may be equalized.

Finally, it should be noted that the distinction between men's and women's language is a symptom of a problem in our culture, not the problem itself. Basically it reflects the fact that men and women are expected to have different interests and different roles, hold different types of conversations, and react differently to other people. This point is made especially clearly and nicely by Roy Miller in his book *The Japanese Language.* Although he is discussing the situation in Japanese—and in Japanese society the roles of men and women are much more rigidly stratified than they are in ours—nevertheless an analogy between what he is saying and what I have said can easily be drawn. Let me reproduce the relevant passage in full:

> Another important part of the system of speech levels is the distinction between men's and women's speech. Partly these differences operate within the larger system of speech levels. For example, women make more use of the deferential prefix *o-* and of elegant and exalted verb

forms than do men, etc., and certain of these aspects have already been touched upon above in our brief summary of the levels system. But sexual differentiation in Japanese also includes different sets of sentence-final particles for men (. . . *zo,* . . . *yo,* . . . *ze,* etc.) and for women (. . . *wa,* . . . *no*), as well as different repertories of interjections for each group. Women also favor variant pronunciations of certain forms (gozămasu for gozaimasu). But in general the differences between men's and women's speech are too far-reaching and too closely interdependent upon content and style to admit of any simple summary. Put most briefly, women in Japanese society traditionally talk about different things than men do, or at the very least, they say different things even when they talk about the same topics. This makes it difficult and even pointless to attempt to give typical equivalent expressions in men's and women's speech, since in most situations the content and topic will differ as much as would the formal verbal expression.

The following brief text is a good example of fairly elegant but otherwise quite run-of-the-mill women's speech:

A. [I am omitting Miller's Japanese dialogue here for convenience, and using only the English translations Miller gives alongside.] My, what a splendid garden you have here—the lawn is so nice and big, it's certainly wonderful, isn't it?

B. Oh no, not at all, we don't take care of it at all any more, so it simply doesn't always look as nice as we would like it to.

A. Oh no, I don't think so at all—but since it's such a big garden, of course it must be quite a tremendous task to take care of it all by yourself; but even so, you certainly do manage to make it look nice all the time: it certainly is nice and pretty any time one sees it.

B. No, I'm afraid not, not at all . . .

This English version, a fairly literal if not word-for-word translation of the Japanese, will make it clear that in every sense this is a very special kind of discourse. What is being said here is not at all important; the only thing of any concern to either speaker is the way in which it is being said, and the number of times the same thing can be repeated. And it is really pointless to ask what the equivalent of all this would be in men's speech, because Japanese men would not carry on in this way about anything, particularly about gardens. A male equivalent text for speaker A would simply be, *ii niwa da ná,* "it's a nice garden, isn't it," and that would be the end of it; to this the reply of speaker B, if any, would most likely be a sub-linguistic grunt, as a sign of acknowledgement or of polite denial.[1]

1. R. A. Miller, *The Japanese Language* (Chicago: University of Chicago Press, 1967), pp. 289–90.

We will return to this point later: it will be seen to be equally valid, if sometimes less striking, in American dialogue. But I think Miller's major point is unquestionably valid: typical "men's talk" is done for a different purpose than typical "women's talk." The differences between the two arise largely out of this.

2 / Forms of Politeness

With these facts in mind, we can return to our original question: Why are women supposed to be more "polite" than men, and why is it considered necessary for men to be more "polite" in the presence of women? And, a related question: If, as is often suggested, politeness is developed by societies in order to reduce friction in personal interaction, why do many feminists feel affronted by these special women-related forms of "politeness," and why do they feel that they must be abolished if true equality between the sexes is ever to be attained?

The fact that different cultures may adjudge the same act in the same circumstances polite or rude indicates that there must be more than one rule of "politeness"—that is, that some cultures will apply one rule preferentially, at a given state in a relationship, where another will apply another. Also we are aware that certain of the ingredients of "politeness" may be combined with one another, or may coexist—others are mutually exclusive. Again, this suggests the existence of several rules, working together or separately as the case may be. Ideally the Rules of Politeness, when fully and correctly formulated, should be able to predict *why,* in a particular culture, a particular act in a particular circumstance is polite, or not polite; and should also be valid for both linguistic polite behavior (saying "please"; using "formal" pronouns in languages that have such forms) and nonlinguistic politeness (opening doors for others; bringing wine to your dinner host). As a first attempt, I suggest three such rules; I feel that at least these three are needed. Although at first glance it seems possible and attractive to compress them into one, closer examination reveals that by doing so we would lose the ability to make predictions of certain kinds about the types of behavior and judgments that occur. The rules are as follows:

1. Formality: keep aloof.
2. Deference: give options.
3. Camaraderie: show sympathy.

The first of these rules is perhaps the one most prominent in etiquette books and other considerations of formal politeness. We see it in those languages that differentiate between a formal and an informal *you:* when the formal *you* is in use, the effect is to create distance between speaker and addressee. Legalese and medicalese, for various reasons known best to their speakers, also utilize this rule in their use of technical terminology. This distances speaker both from addressee and from what he is saying, implying that there is no emotive content to his utterance, and thus the participants can remain aloof. In this way, it is wise to talk about *carcinoma* rather than *cancer,* which carries unpleasant emotional connotations. By using these terms, the doctor (or anyone who uses jargon, including of course all of us academics) maintains both distance from and superiority over his addressee. Another example is what might be called the Academic Passive: "In this paper it has been shown. . . ." Neophyte authors are often advised to use active sentences: the reason is that the active voice indicates involvement on the part of the speaker or writer, and thereby invites the participation, or sympathy, of the reader or hearer. But if you want to appear cool and above it all, you use the passive, and this is what academics are prone to do. Another such device is the academic-authorial *we* (in papers by a single author), parallel in function to the plural *vous* (as opposed to *tu*) in French, and to be distinguished from the various other non-first-person plural *we*'s (the editorial and royal *we;* the *we* reserved for talking to children, as in "Now let's tie our shoes, and then we'll take a nice nap").

Hypercorrect forms and avoidance of colloquialism are another means of achieving distance, and the use of titles (Mr., Dr., Sir, and so on) plus last name still another. Nonlinguistically, formal dress, which is always uncomfortable and generally concealing, plays just this role.

One final example of the use of Rule 1 is the impersonal pronoun *one,* particularly when used as a substitute for *you* or *I.* To Americans, the British seem especially devoted to Rule 1 politeness, and one indication of their addiction to this rule is, in fact, the many ways in which *one* may be used in standard British English, and not in American English at all: "One feels awful about that" seems, if I read novels by British authors correctly, to be the translational equivalent of "I feel awful about that." I think I have also seen in British novels dialogue such as "One shouldn't have done that now, should one?" as an admonition to a second person.

The second rule, that of deference, may be used alone or in combination with either of the other two rules, while Rule 1 and Rule 3 are mutually exclusive. The application of this rule makes it look as though the option as to how to behave, or what to do, is being left up to the addressee. Of course, this is very often mere sham or convention, when the speaker knows very well that he has the power to enforce a decision. Most forms of Rule 1 behavior tend to suggest that the speaker's social status is superior to that of the addressee; generally Rule 2 politeness conveys, whether really or conventionally, the superiority of the addressee over the speaker. Examples of Rule 2: hesitancy in speech and action generally. Question intonation and tag questioning are Rule 2 related devices as long as the speaker is not really uncertain about the truth of his assertion. Hedges, similarly, work this way: they leave the addressee the option of deciding how seriously to take what the speaker is saying. It is for this reason that "John is sorta short" may be, in the right context, a polite way of saying "John is short," rather than a scaled-down comment on John's actual height.

Finally, and parallel to the use of technical terms that was cited above as a Rule 1 device, we find euphemisms used in accordance with Rule 2. They are similar in that both skirt an issue, and thus are ways of discussing a touchy subject while pretending to be doing something else. But technical terms evade the issue by saying, in effect: Well, this would be touchy if we were emotionally involved, but no, we are remote, so touchiness doesn't arise. Euphemisms grant that the subject is touchy, but pretend that *it* is not the matter under discussion. Hence we find academic writing replete with technical terms when it is objectivity and scholarly aloofness that is desired; but we find cocktail party chitchat full of euphemisms, since when we gossip we aren't after remoteness, but we do want to avoid offense by avoiding coming head on with ideas that may not be fully palatable when made explicit. Thus, neither the doctor writing on sexual practices in a learned text nor the hostess talking about the doings of her friends to mutual friends might want to use the straight four-letter word that most directly describes the situation. So the doctor expounds: *"Copulation* may also be enhanced by the use of oleaginous materials," and the hostess gushes, "Selma told me she found Jimmy and Marion *doing it* with mayonnaise!" Euphemisms, then, are Rule 2 related because they allow the addressee the option of seeming not to be hearing what he actually is hearing, although again the pretense is conventional: both speaker and addressee know full well what it is that they are discussing, or else, of course, the discussion would founder, as it occasionally does when the euphemisms become too thick or too arcane for perception.

The third rule is sometimes said not to be part of politeness; but in American society, gestures of friendliness are certainly considered in this category; it is only in (Rule 1 linked) formal etiquette treatises that the two are not connected, and this is as we would expect, since as I said, Rule 1 and Rule 3 are mutually exclusive. You cannot be extending the hand of friendship and stepping back aloofly at once. But you can combine Rule 3 with Rule 2: you can be friendly and deferential, just as you can combine Rules 1 and 2, to be aloof but deferential. As we shall see, how many and which of the rules you apply in a given situation are determined by your subculture as well as by your personal psychological makeup.

The purpose of Rule 3 is to make the addressee feel that the speaker likes him and wants to be friendly with him, is interested in him, and so on. Like the other rules it can be real or conventional. For instance, backslapping is a well-known nonlinguistic Rule 3 device. And it can be done where real camaraderie is felt, for instance, between friends, one of whom is glad to see the other after a long absence; or it can be done by a salesman to a (male) prospect, concurrent with telling him dirty jokes, another Rule 3 related device, and here conventional again. Colloquial language generally is Rule 3 linked, as is the use of four-letter words, rather than either the technical terms of Rule 1 or the euphemisms of Rule 2. Saying the thing directly conveys to the addressee: We're in this together, we understand each other, we don't have to stand on ceremony with each other. Finally, the use of nicknames and first name alone in some conditions, last name alone in others, is a Rule 3 device. The first two rules tend to occur where inequality between speaker and hearer exists or may exist; the third implies full egalitarianism. Of course, problems may arise, as they often do in a college class where the professor invites the students to call him (or her) by first name. The students sense that this equality is conventional, since the professor clearly has perquisites they do not possess; and further, if they attempt to extend the invitation to include other Rule 3 devices (like backslapping or friendly teasing) they may be in for a big surprise when the friendship suddenly cools.

It should be clear by now that three separate rules are needed to arrive even at a minimal definition of politeness (and clearly there are plenty of residual problems, which I will not worry about here). So a tag question when used for politeness is purely in the realm of Rule 2, but the use of *please* in a request involves both Rule 1 (the speaker is indicating some distance) and Rule 2 (he is acting probably conventionally as though the addressee might refuse). And an injunction like "You wanna screw, baby?" has elements of both Rule 2 and Rule 3. But combining Rules 1 and 3 seems unlikely: we might end up with: "Wanna screw, Professor Jones?" or perhaps: "Wanna copulate, baby?"

It should be evident too that different cultures consider these rules of different priority, or applicable under different conditions. So, for example, let us consider the case of belching after a meal in public. Standard American society frowns on this; classical Chinese society, on the other hand, considers it the polite thing to do. Can our rules account for the way these two cultures behave?

Here we have a situation that might be viewed in either of two ways. You might feel that any internal physical process, made explicit and evident to the outside world, was an intrusion on other people's privacy. So you would attempt to suppress or conceal any such act in public. Not only is belching thought of this way, but so are sneezing and coughing (etiquette manuals warned people to cover their mouths when performing these acts long before the germ theory of disease was known). Thus you don't remove food from your mouth after you've chewed it, or wipe your nose on your sleeve (where the evidence that you did so will remain in full view of others). All these are violations of Rule 1. Of course, you can violate Rule 2 at the same time, and make matters even worse: it's not good manners to spit in your soup at a dinner party, but it's unspeakable to spit in your neighbor's, thus denying him his autonomy.

But there are other ways of viewing a belch. You might think of it as an expression of repletion, indicating satisfaction with the quality and quantity of the feast, the more powerful because it is (supposedly) involuntary. (Of course, in Chinese society, I would not be surprised if the conventionalized artificial belch existed, rather like our artificial yawn.) In this case, belching is viewed as an application of Rule 3— you have said something nice to your host, made him feel appreciated. So how you categorize a particular act may determine whether it is to be considered polite according to one rule, or rude according to another.

Or it may be that there is an order of precedence among the rules, determining which is preferentially applied at various points in a relationship, and this may differ between cultures. I am suggesting here that the rules as stated are universal: in no society, it is my preliminary prediction, will there be *no* reflexes of any of these rules; but one society may apply Rule 1 every chance it gets, to the very advanced stages of intimacy, and another will switch to Rule 3 with unimaginable celerity. When members of these two hypothetical cultures meet, it is analogous to the meeting of matter and antimatter: an explosion takes place. This happens all the time: one speaker says something meant to indicate warmth and friendship; the second speaker backs away, ending the exchange abruptly, muttering, "He has some nerve!" The first speaker wanders off, musing, "Now what's the matter with *him?*"

Consider what happens when an American, a German, and a Japanese meet. Suppose they all want to make a good impression and to be "polite" according to their own standards. Chances are, unless the members of the group are very sophisticated and have had prior exposure to the other cultures, the American will seem to the others overly brash, familiar, and prying; the Japanese will seem cloyingly deferential; the German will seem distant and uninterested in the others to the point of arrogance. So they will part, each thinking the others are thoroughly detestable because of individual personality defects. And if each meets other members of the other cultures chances are these first impressions will be reinforced, until national stereotypes are formed: Americans are "too personal"; Japanese are "too humble"; Germans are "too stiff." Actually, what is happening is that each is conforming to a cultural stereotype of what constitutes polite behavior toward a slight acquaintance. At this stage of a relationship, a German will emphasize Rule 1, a Japanese Rule 2, and an American Rule 3. (These are of course the stereotypical norms; there are plenty of participants in these cultures whose rule application, for various idiosyncratic reasons, is different.) Now as a relationship increases in familiarity, the Japanese will start moving toward the incorporation of Rule 3 along with his Rule 2; so he will always, probably, seem a bit more deferential than an American will, but ultimately he will seem *friendly* and deferential. The German, after a suitable interval of acquaintanceship, will gradually drop the Rule 1 related devices and start acquiring the forms of Rule 3, but it will take him some time. So it is not that the three cultures have three different rules as to how to be polite; it's just that they have different conditions on the applicability of the three rules they share.

As Miller noted in the excerpt given above, conversations in which politeness is a major criterion for acceptability are of a special kind: they don't seek to impart real-world information, but rather are largely engaged in for the purpose of communicating one's own feelings about one's addressee, and garnering some intuition about his feelings toward one. So it isn't important what you say, really, but rather how you say it, and, perhaps, also, why you say it. If I say, "It's cold out," to someone who is hesitating as to which of two coats to put on, I am probably expressing real-world information primarily; but if I say it to someone I have just met at a bus stop, no information is being communicated (since he knows it's cold as well as I do); rather, I'm trying to interact with him and form a friendship, however short-lived. In the first instance, politeness is not involved; in the second, we might say I was engaged in a Rule 3 type of situation since I was principally expressing a desire for acquaintanceship.

This is an important point, since we shall find it useful to separate the rules by which we structure polite utterances, and decide whether they are appropriate, from the parallel sorts of rules we use for deciding the contextual appropriateness of utterances in circumstances when politeness is not at issue. In the latter cases, we seek to communicate *information:* to apprise an addressee of information we have, but he does not have and needs to know, by the least circuitous route. If we are concerned with the pure transmission of factual knowledge, any communication that does not meet the criteria just listed will be an aberrant or failed communication, while if we are talking for some other purpose, the same utterance may be eminently successful.

A system of rules by which factual information may best be conveyed has been proposed by H. P. Grice in his paper "The Logic of Conversation." In this work, Grice proposes four basic Rules of Conversation, which we can summarize as follows:

1. Quality. Say only what is true.
2. Quantity. Say only as much, and just as much, as is necessary.
3. Relevance. Be relevant.
4. Manner. Be perspicuous. Don't be ambiguous. Don't be obscure. Be succinct.

Clearly these rules, like the Rules of Politeness proposed earlier, leave much to be desired in terms of specificity: how does one tell if a potential conversational contribution is "relevant"? "Necessary"? But they are useful guidelines. Grice also notices that a great deal of actual conversation is in violation of these rules, yet is not normally considered aberrant, nor is there usually any problem in understanding the force or purpose of such nonconforming contributions. He gives as one example the case of a letter of recommendation for a fellowship that states: "Miss X has nice handwriting." Now at first glance, this is a violation of quantity and/or relevance. It is not necessary to know about a fellowship candidate's handwriting in order to judge if the candidate is worthy of receiving support. What Grice says is that, by its very (apparent) irrelevance, the statement implies something else, approximately: "On a fellowship recommendation one is supposed to say only favorable things about the candidate. Well, this is the only point in Miss X's favor that I know of. *Ergo,* this statement implies another: 'Miss X does not deserve to get the fellowship, since she has no relevant good qualities.' " This is what Grice refers to as a conversational implicature.

The important question for us here is: Why (or when) is it useful to use implicature? Why not always speak logically, directly, and to the point?

Here we have a situation in which the rules of conversation would come into conflict with one or more of the rules of politeness. We have a violation of the third rule of politeness, applied indirectly; that is, to say what we have to say explicitly would be making Miss X look bad, and feel bad, if she knew. There is a colloquial principle that expresses this notion: "If you can't say something nice, don't say anything at all." A clearer illustration of the conflict can be found in cases in which it is the addressee whose feelings would be directly impinged upon. So I might say, "It's cold in here," and mean by it any of the following:

1. Why didn't you close the window?
2. You borrowed my favorite sweater.
3. Let's go into another room.
4. You're going to make me catch cold.

And so on. Now, saying any of 1–4 will violate some rule of politeness, probably 2 or 3 or a combination. Generally, implicature seems to be used as a Rule 2 related device: a means of letting the addressee have the benefit of the doubt, come to his own conclusions (again, often merely by convention, since there is usually only one meaning to be derived from the utterance). So we can say that Grice's Conversational Principles are usable only in case there is no possibility of conflict with the Rules of Politeness, or in situations in which polite conversation is not felt to be required, where pure information is to be transmitted, information about the outside world, rather than about the personal and interpersonal feelings of the speaker and the addressee. And, consequently, the less speaker and addressee wish to communicate about their personal feelings, the more likely it is that the Rules of Conversation will be in effect, permitting the participants in the discourse to say what they need to say, and stop there. So Rule 1 type politeness is consonant with application of the Rules of Conversation; but Rule 2 and 3 politeness situations call for the use of statements whose meaning is derivable by the notion of conversational implicature.

So, to paraphrase Miller again, what you are talking about has a great deal of influence on how you will say it: directly and straight, or indirectly and repetitiously. The former exemplifies the strict use of Grice's principles, the latter of conversational implicature. We may also note that it is among the misogynistic stereotypes in our culture that women cannot follow the rules of conversation: that a woman's discourse is necessarily indirect, repetitious, meandering, unclear, exaggerated—the antithesis of every one of Grice's principles—while of course a man's speech is clear, direct, precise, and to the point. Now obviously to hold this belief literally is idiotic, since everyone knows plenty of women who habitually speak straighter than plenty of men. But, as I remarked earlier, stereotypes are not to be ignored: first, because for a stereotype to exist, it must be an exaggeration of something that is in fact in existence and able to be recognized; and second, because one measures oneself, for better or worse, according to how well or poorly one conforms to the stereotype one is supposed to conform to.

3 / Women and Politeness

Another, less value-laden way of looking at things is to say that the stereotyped image of men's speech is that it functions in accord with the rules of conversation, and of women's speech, that it tends to make wider use of the properties of implicature. There is no particular reason to suppose that there is extra virtue inherent in the men's way: if people think so, it is because men in this culture tend to impose their value judgments on everyone, so that the men's way of doing things becomes the "good way," and the women's way the bad way. It would be better to think of the situation in these terms: there are two possible conversational styles (with, of course, infinite possibilities for mixtures and intersections); one style tends to predominate in men's speech, another in women's. This might be true in either of two ways: more men might habitually adopt one style usually, more women the other; or, men in general would tend to use more of one style, though sometimes falling into the other; and the same with women. The latter seems to be the truth that underlies the stereotype. In general and in traditional American culture (we are not talking about academia here, for reasons already noted) women will tend to speak with reference to the rules of politeness, conversational implicature, and interpersonal exploration; men will tend to speak with reference to the rules of conversation and straight factual communication. It seems to be true of both men and women, however, that when the crunch comes, the rules of politeness will supersede the rules of conversation: better be unclear than rude.

If this is a viable hypothesis, there is a relationship among several things that are stated to be generally true of women: they are more interested in interpersonal discovery than in discussion of external things; and women are ladies, more polite than men are. The first creates the second, and the second no doubt expedites the first in turn.

Again, it is important to remember that neither of these two styles is good or bad: each is valuable in its own context. But men and women both err if they cannot switch readily from one style to the other as the situation warrants. It may be that the traditional woman could not easily switch styles when necessary, and the stereotype is true in that sense; but it is equally true that the traditional man cannot switch out of his straight-from-the-shoulder pose; and this is just as damaging. But, as with jokes as we shall see below, men make up the stereotypes, and groups typically don't invent stereotypes about themselves, but about other groups. Hence it is the dominant group in a society that establishes stereotypes of the other groups, and decides which groups, on the basis of these stereotypes, are "good" and "bad." The job of people who find themselves, as members of nondominant groups, being stereotyped is not necessarily to decide that there is no truth underlying the stereotype and that therefore the stereotype is bad and must be destroyed (though this may sometimes be true); but it may also be worthwhile to assume that there is some truth behind the stereotype, but that what it represents is a good trait rather than the bad one it had been assumed by the dominant group to be. Women sometimes realize this: thus, it had been axiomatic in our culture for some time that women lacked aggressiveness and that this was a bad thing about women, a reason why they'd never make it in the real world, and never had. Women had two possible options for dealing with this stereotype: to deny it, proving they were just as pugnacious as men, or to reaffirm it and take nonaggressiveness to be a virtue. Different groups have done different things in this regard, but certainly the latter position is a strong one. We must not continue to be brainwashed.

We may ask how these two styles establish themselves as sex-linked traits. Is it inherent, and thus inevitable? Or is it learned at an early age? Evidence for the latter is that some women don't learn the predominant female style; this is a hopeful augury, since we might eventually learn how to educate all children to be equally fluent in both speech types. The distinction appears at a very early age: psychologists studying children in nursery school have found that little boys already tend to communicate about external things—building garages, having battles, and so on—while little girls are more apt to talk about their own and other people's feelings, about each other, and about their socialization patterns (who is best friends with whom, and so on). As mentioned previously, other studies have shown that little girls are "politer" in speech than boys of the same age, so we may assume that these two styles of behavior are learned together, as we would expect.

Another question raised at the outset of this discussion has not yet been answered: Not only are women more polite, but men are supposed to be more polite around women than they are with each other;

further, this sort of politeness is problematic: if the purpose of politeness is to decrease friction and promote friendship, why does men-to-women politeness so often seem offensive or constraining? If politeness is supposed to bring people closer together, allowing them to interact more easily with one another, why does this special kind of politeness seem so exclusive—why do women resent the sudden hush that sweeps over a roomful of men when it is realized that "there are ladies present"?

I think that the feeling of exclusiveness produced by men-to-women politeness is not imaginary, and I think that examining it will lead us to some interesting conclusions. We might note, first off, that there is no comparable exclusive female tactic: there's no conversational style you are supposed to drop when a man enters the room. (There are tabooed *topics*, of course, mostly sexual, or rather, gynecological: women go along with men's assumption that female sexual anatomy is particularly revolting.)

On the basis of ethological studies on primates, a theory has been proposed that, while unattractive in many ways and certainly open to criticism in several of its aspects, nevertheless if taken not totally literally offers a means of understanding some of the strange and rather paradoxical things that seem to be going on. This is the notion of male bonding, as proposed by such anthropologists as Lionel Tiger, in his book *Men in Groups*. Tiger says that in primates the males often seem to have the task of hunting together in groups for food, while the females stay behind, functioning as individuals, caring for the young. He hypothesizes that this general situation necessarily pertained in groups of primitive human beings, at least until the advent of agriculture: the men hunted together in packs, while the women stayed behind, caring for their individual living sites and raising the children. Now in order to hunt successfully—particularly since man had only primitive weapons, and was not very strong or swift in comparison with his prey—the male members of the tribe had to work together, develop effective techniques of cooperation, and learn to enjoy one another's company and minimize interpersonal friction. The women, since they worked largely alone—or, if they chose to work together, they did not cooperate at one single task as the men did, but rather each did her individual job in the company of others —did not need to develop techniques of working as a group. Now obviously, within the male group, some members might be singled out as, say, the best archers or the fleetest runners; so that within the general atmosphere of cooperation you might find competition; but basically the males directed their efforts toward a common goal; among the females, each had her own goal and succeeded as an individual. Of course, having no records of human life in those primitive times, we have no means of knowing whether this theory is correct; but Tiger discusses some characteristics of modern life that might be viewed as stemming from those habits inculcated in the species millennia ago. In this view, it is the present-day reflexes of male bonding that enable men to work together in industry, politics, religion, the military—any powerful group, to retain its power, must have some sort of cohesive force underlying it, inducing its members to work as a team. And indeed, in virtually every culture we look at, we see that men are in control of all the major institutions. (Margaret Mead and others have discussed a few isolated societies in which women seem to be in charge, but these are small in size and few in number—and indeed, we may even have reason to believe that the lack of success of these societies is in part due to the fact that women are in control. Certainly such cultures represent aberrations from the norm.) Tiger suggests that these groups work by relying on male bonding, and that this is in fact why women find it so hard to be accepted as members, why in fact often they opt out entirely: they feel they are out of place. Further, this is why men like to go on "stag" hunting and fishing trips, and generally congregate in all-male groups. There are occasional exceptions, and of course the more a society is able to divest itself of millennia-old habits, the more women will be integrated into the formerly all-male groups. If people can become vegetarians, or avoid war, they presumably can compensate for the reflexes of male bonding; but none of these departures from the age-old norms is very widespread in society as yet.

This thesis is viewed with alarm by many feminists, principally because it seems to suggest that things are hopeless: "This is an ingrained habit," such a theory suggests, "and you'll never change it, because it goes deeper than the roots of the human race." Certainly that is the position Tiger holds. But it is not necessary to accept such a pessimistic point of view. One can, as a feminist, agree that there is something going on in the overwhelming majority of cultures today that can be described as "male bonding," and may want to agree, too, that this goes back as far into recorded history as we can see, and, from primate evidence, perhaps back to the very dawn of mankind. But man has changed much about himself: from (probably) an original fruit eater, he has become an omnivore; from a tree dweller, a ground animal; and so on. We might work toward either of two goals: to reduce the necessity for bonding among men, or to encourage it among women, and among all people. Or we might try all these options, mitigating men's desire to bond, and strengthening women's. Considering the changes that have occurred only in the past decade in our views on, say, sexual normality, it doesn't seem too far-fetched that our views on the ways, necessity, and pleasures of bonding might be similarly altered, if people set their minds to it, before too long. Never underestimate the influence of the media.

We would like, that is, not only for men to accept women as integral parts of their groups, but for women to be able to group with other women as men do with men. As Phyllis Chesler points out, this is not at present normally the case:

> Women, although similar to each other in many ways, are more isolated from each other *in terms of groups* [italics hers] than men are. Women are not consolidated into either public or powerful groups. Women as mothers are "grouped" with their children (who grow up and leave them), and only temporarily, and superficially with other women: for example, in parks, at women's auxiliary functions, and at heterosexual parties.[2]

I think that a start is being made, in women's groups, to overcome this tendency of women not to bond. The women's movement, in referring to and addressing women universally as "sisters," is working to establish a sense of female camaraderie, though it is still a camara-

2. Phyllis Chesler, *Women and Madness* (New York: Doubleday & Co., 1972), p. 270.

derie of the underdog, just as a WASP male doesn't think of himself as a "brother" of other WASP males, but a black male will consider himself a "brother" of other black males. "Sister" really means something like: "You who are one with me in our oppression," rather than merely being an expression of pure unity. It is in any case a good beginning. But perhaps even more important, for women and for the human race generally, is establishing patterns of bonding between both sexes, so that women, with their special abilities, sensitivities, and talents, may be integrated into the "real world"; and men, with theirs, may learn to function more smoothly in the home.

The notion of bonding, if we can accept the fact that something of the sort occurs in present-day American traditional society, can also serve to explain some of our findings about politeness. We can see that Rule 1 acts as a kind of discourager of bonding, saying as it does: Keep away. Rule 3, on the other hand, encourages bonding relationships. (Rule 2 would seem to be able to reinforce the effect of either Rule 1 or Rule 3.) We have noted that women's politeness is principally of the Rule 1 plus Rule 2 type, establishing and reinforcing distance: deferential mannerisms coupled with euphemism and hypercorrect and superpolite usage. Women's language avoids the markers of camaraderie: backslapping, joke telling, nicknaming, slang, and so forth. In all-female groups, we find devices that recall male intimacy-creating gestures: embraces for backslapping, discussion of personal things. But in mixed groups, *all* manifestations of camaraderie disappear: this is really the principal problem: why in mixed groups there is nothing identifiable as Rule 3 behavior. (Again I am talking about traditional society.) And even in all-women groups, my impression is that typically there is less show of camaraderie than in all-men groups. Perhaps more interestingly, the women's type of camaraderie seems less able to be used conventionally: men can tell dirty jokes and slap each other's backs even when they can't stand each other; this is presumably how a great deal of the world's work gets done. But women embrace and share confidences only when there are real feelings of sympathy between them.

One counterexample that has been suggested to me is the use of words like "dear," "honey," "luv," and so forth between people who are not sexually or emotionally intimate. Interestingly, both sexes may engage in it, between or within sex lines. But it still seems that women use these expressions under different conditions than men do. Women who are socially subordinate may use it to either men or women: saleswomen and waitresses are particularly apt to do this. But men (heterosexual males, that is) don't use it to other men at all; and when they use it to women, the woman is definitely in an inferior position. I have known male professors who habitually addressed their female students as "dear," but I have never heard of a female professor addressing her male students thus. (It is barely conceivable that an elderly female professor might so address favorite female students, though I know of no such instances; I can't imagine her addressing a male student that way, though.) Doctors and dentists (male) and especially, I am told, gynecologists are prone to address their female (never male) patients this way; patients may never respond in kind. This is probably related to the fact that men generally feel free to address women by first name alone or nickname much sooner in a relationship than a woman will feel free to so address a male. This is sometimes justified by the user on grounds of "friendship"; but if first name alone is not mutual, we have a relationship not of Rule 3 solidarity but rather one of Rule 1 class distinction, in which the person who is addressed by first name is considered inferior to the one who is not. Compare, for example, the forms of normal address between adults and children, particularly primary school children and their teachers.

Since "dear" and its cohorts are not mutually exchanged, we must assume that a nonparallel relationship exists—as it always does between doctor and patient anyway, but the more markedly when the patient is female.

Then this aspect of the "ladyship" of women may be explained through the concept of male bonding: male politeness is different from female and mixed politeness, in that male politeness makes use of Rule 3 to encourage bonding relationships, and the others do not, and thus discourage them. It is for this reason that women feel excluded by male-type "polite" behavior toward them. Men, in effect, say: "Stay away: our friendship doesn't include you."

A particularly striking instance of the way this principle operates may be seen in joke-telling behavior. A joke is generally considered "tasteful" when it will not offend anyone who is likely to hear it. It is the definition of "anyone" which has changed of late and could use some more changing. Usually we mean "anyone who counts." The reason we tell jokes is to become part of a (Rule 3 governed) bonding relationship. Really or conventionally, joke telling brings the teller and the hearers together. You are nervous to some extent while a joke is being told: as the teller, for fear you'll get it wrong; as the hearer, for fear you won't get it. Both of these possible responses are dangerous because they would inhibit the formation of the bond, making it difficult or impossible for hearer and teller to relate satisfactorily to each other. But if the joke is offensive to someone in the audience, it is guaranteed that the teller will fail in his intention to establish a bond, at least for that person. And when a teller is confronting a huge audience, in the media, then of course he can't tell how many members of the insultable groups might be out there listening: he can't jeopardize his chances of establishing bonding relationships by telling jokes that might offend a sizable portion of his audience.

In the past, it was implicitly assumed that members of various outside groups were not available for bonding with members of other groups. So if you were a WASP, it was all right to tell anti-anybody else jokes; if you were Jewish, you could tell anti-Irish or anti-black jokes, and so on. But lately we have become more sensitive: we have included, at least for the purpose of conventional bond establishing (as opposed to real camaraderie) all ethnic groups among the "anybody" who cannot be offended, at the risk of ruining the effect of the joke.

There is, however, one group that does not comprise part of the "anybody," from all available evidence. This is not a minority, but is usually about half of any audience. That group is, of course, women. There is a whole genre of antiwomen jokes, based on sexual stereotypes as antiethnic jokes were (and are) based on ethnic stereotypes: women as a group and any woman because of belonging to that group are vain, fuzzy-minded, extravagant, imprecise, long-winded . . . and numerous variants on those themes, concerning jealousy of other women, hat buying, driving, and so on. There are to my knowledge no parallel joke types based on stereotypes of men in general. Even female comediennes don't tell such jokes, probably because men make up the jokes, or at least men seem to establish what constitutes acceptable topics for joking about.

A comedian may be very sensitive to ethnic slurs, never be caught dead telling Polish jokes, anti-Semitic jokes, or any of the other no-no's, but he will include lots of antiwomen (these days, anti-"women's lib") jokes in his repertoire. No one (with the exception of a few of those chronic female malcontents who obviously have no sense of humor) will be offended, and generally the women in the audience will laugh as loud as the men. (They'd better, or they'll be accused of typical female humorlessness or stupidity because they "don't get it.") I think considerable damage is done to malleable young female egos in this way: jokes are not harmless, as ethnic minorities are fully aware. This sort of reaction to antiwomen jokes shows that women are not expected, by men or by themselves, to be among the possible people to participate in the bonding induced by joke telling. And it is related to this that women are notorious for not being able to tell jokes well: this is often ascribed to their illogical habits of mind, but probably has at least as much to do with the fact that women don't, can't, gain from telling jokes: in fact, in many circles it's considered a dangerous sign of nonfemininity if a woman *can* tell a real joke (not merely recount an anecdote) without lousing up.

At first glance, there may seem to be a paradox implicit in the claims I have made, namely:

1. That women are person-oriented, interested in their own and each other's mental states and respective status; men are object-oriented, interested in things in the outside world.

2. That men enter into bonding relationships and form relationships of camaraderie, in a way that they do not with women, nor do women really with one another.

But actually there is no paradox. In looking at each other's psyches, and reactions to one another, women retain their individuality; they are not fused into a group. There is not necessarily a sense of cooperation in this process, but rather a sense that each individual is keeping track of the other individuals. In this sense, women's greater ability to express and share emotions is less to be ascribed to camaraderie than to separateness, one individual getting and giving impressions from and to other individuals, and as a means whereby individuals can come to work together when needed.

Men, on the other hand, are not so much concerned about what's going on in one another's minds, but rather on how the group can work as a whole to get something done. This leads to the submerging of everyone's feelings and some gruffness of reaction, of course, which the rules producing camaraderie are expressly set up to help gloss over.

Again, there should be no sense on reading this that one style is *better,* more logical, or more socially useful than another; both, and mixtures of both, are needed in different circumstances. Women must be more flexible—and so must men.

4 / Conclusion

This, then, is finally the point for the reader to ponder: I have given reason to believe that the kinds of "politeness" used by and of and to women do not arise by accident; that they are, indeed, stifling, exclusive, and oppressive. But I don't feel that we must maintain the kinds of social relationships we have always assumed. If we are aware of what we're doing, why we're doing it, and the effects our actions have on ourselves and everyone else, we will have the power to change. I hope this book will be one small first step in the direction of a wider option of life styles, for men and women.

Bibliography

Bateson, G. *Steps to an Ecology of Mind,* Part III: "Form and Pathology in Relationship." New York: Ballantine, 1972.

Chesler, Phyllis. *Women and Madness.* New York: Doubleday & Co., 1972; Avon paperback, 1973.

Grice, H. P. "The Logic of Conversation." Unpublished manuscript, Department of Philosophy, University of California, Berkeley, 1968.

Haas, M. R. "Men's and Women's Speech in Loasati," in D. Hymes, ed., *Language in Culture and Society.* New York: Harper & Row, 1964.

Lakoff, R. "Language in Context." *Language* 48 (1972): 907–27.

Miller, R. A. *The Japanese Language.* Chicago: University of Chicago Press, 1967.

Postal, P. "Anaphoric Islands." In *Papers from the Fifth Regional Meeting of the Chicago Linguistic Society,* edited by R. Binnick et al. Chicago: Chicago Linguistic Society, 1969.

Tiger, Lionel. *Men in Groups.* London: Thomas Nelson & Sons, Ltd., and New York: Random House, 1969; Vintage paperback, 1970.